Herbert Puchta · Peter Lewis-Jones · Günter Gerngross · Catherine Zgouras

CAMBRIDGE
UNIVERSITY PRESS

Contents

Meet the Explorers

1 🎧 **001** Listen and write the numbers.

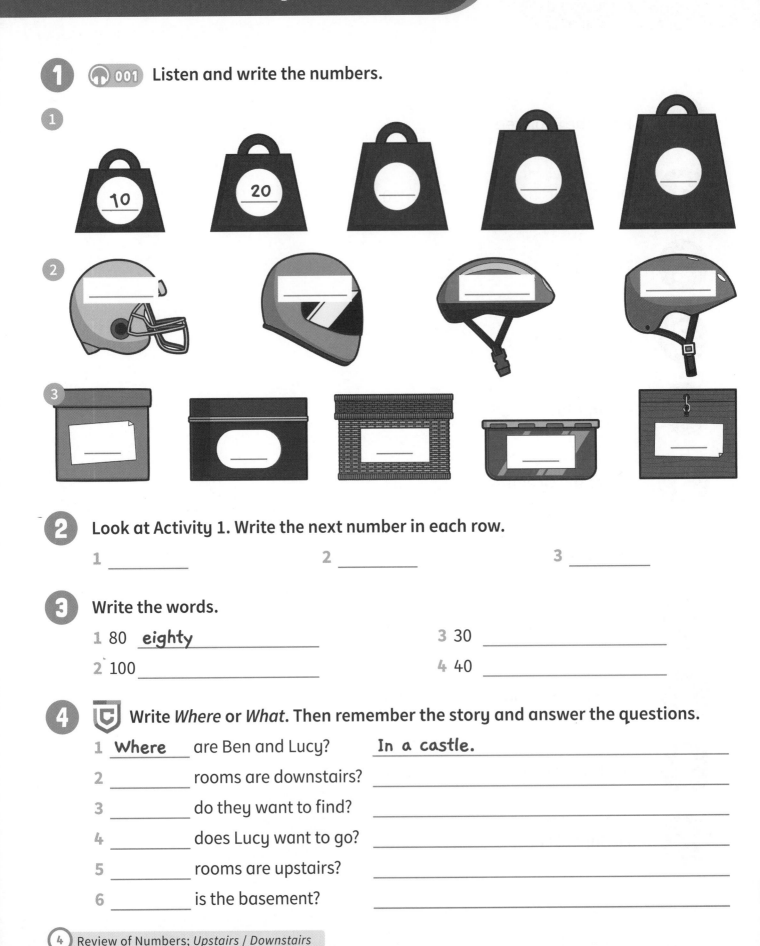

1

10   20   ___   ___   ___

2

3

2 Look at Activity 1. Write the next number in each row.

1 _____   2 _____   3 _____

3 Write the words.

1 80 _eighty_____   3 30 _____

2 100 _____   4 40 _____

4 🛡 Write *Where* or *What*. Then remember the story and answer the questions.

1 **Where** are Ben and Lucy?   In a castle._____

2 _____ rooms are downstairs?   _____

3 _____ do they want to find?   _____

4 _____ does Lucy want to go?   _____

5 _____ rooms are upstairs?   _____

6 _____ is the basement?   _____

1 What are the children good at? Write sentences with *good at* or *not good at*.

	jumping	snorkeling	swimming
Lucas	✓	✗	✓
Olivia	✓	✓	✗

1 Lucas: **I'm good at jumping.**
2 Lucas: _____
3 Lucas: _____

4 Olivia: _____
5 Olivia: _____
6 Olivia: _____

2 Look, think, and draw lines.

He's good at playing soccer.

She's good at dancing.

He's not good at swimming.

She's not good at jumping high.

3 Write about you.

1 **I'm good at speaking English.**
2 _____
3 _____
4 _____

1 Number the lines in each verse 1 to 4. Then write *Ben* or *Lucy*.

___ And reads them very carefully.
___ She always finds the clues
___ They tell her what to do.
1 She's good at doing puzzles.

_____

___ And swimming in the ocean.
___ Just like you and me.
___ He's good at riding horses
___ He's an action hero.

_____

2 Read Emily's new verse. Look and write the words.

1   2   3   4

I'm good at (1) __doing__ puzzles.
I'm good at (2) _____ trees.
I'm not good at (3) _____.
Come on and (4) _____ with me!

Emily

3 Now write a verse about you. Then draw.

I'm good at _____.

I'm _____ at playing soccer.

I'm not good at _____.

That's me, and that is all!

1 🎧 **002** **Listen and write the words.**

son daughter grandmother ~~grandfather~~ grandparents aunt uncle parents

1 Matthew is Simon's **grandfather**.
2 Oliver is Simon's _____.
3 June and Dave are Simon's _____.
4 Gina is Simon's _____.

5 Linda is Maria's _____.
6 Dawn is Maria's _____.
7 Claudia and John are Maria's _____.
8 Thomas is Maria's _____.

2 🛡 **Follow the lines and write about Simon and Maria.**

Joe
(grandfather)

Simon

Maria

Mike
(brother)

Jeremy and
Dorothy
(cousins)

Alice
(grandmother)

Nicholas (son)

Harriet
(sister)

Simon
He's Alice's grandson.
_____
_____

Maria
She's Nicholas's mother.
_____
_____

3 **Look at Activity 2. Write about a person in your family.**

_____
_____
_____

1 **Read the story *The Old Book* again. Then write.**

> get the book back ~~in a castle~~ helps the children can see
> take the book has an idea behind a secret door

1 Lucy and Ben are _in a castle_____.

2 They find the book _____.

3 Horax and Zelda _____ them.

4 They _____ away from the children.

5 Lucy _____.

6 Buster _____ and stops Horax and Zelda.

7 The children _____.

2 Look at the pictures from the story. Read, think, and circle.

How does Ben feel when he says,
"It looks really old!"?
(excited) / bored

How does Horax feel when he says,
"You're good at finding things that I want!"?
happy / sad

In picture 5, do Ben and Lucy know
where the book is?
yes / no

Why does Zelda say, "Go away, silly
dog!" in picture 7?
She **likes / doesn't like** Buster.

1 Color the bricks to make sentences. Write in the missing words.

1	I'm not	playing	riding a bike.
2	Are you _____ at	at _____	French.
3	Ben	good _at_	puzzles?
4	He's not good	is Lucy'____	the piano?
5	Is he	good at _____	friend.

2 Look and write a, e, i, o, or u.

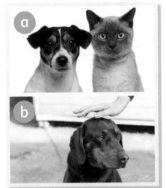  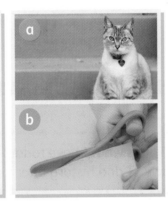 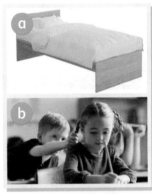

1 a p<u>e</u>ts b p<u>a</u>ts   2 a p_nk b p_n   3 a c_t b c_t   4 a b_d b b_d

3 003 **Listen, say, and check your answers.**

 4 🛡 **Read. Then write about you and draw.**

I'm good at swimming and playing tennis. _____
I'm not good at singing and drawing. _____
_____ _____

1 Our School

1 Read, think, and write the days.

MONDAY	TUESDAY	WEDNESDAY	THURSDAY	FRIDAY
$4+2=6$	💻💻	$4+2=6$	📖 Hello.	📖 Hello.
📖 Hello.	🌐🗺	📖 Hello.	$4+2=6$	⚔
🌐🗺	🎵🎵	⚽🎾	⚗	$4+2=6$
LUNCH				
⚔	🎨⚽	💻💻	🌐🗺	🎵🎵
⚽🎾	⚽🎾	⚔	⚽🎾	⚗

1. This is what I have today. Math, English, and PE before lunch. IT and history after lunch. Today is **Wednesday**.

2. This is what I have today. English, history, and math before lunch. Music and science after lunch. Today is _____.

3. This is what I have today. Math, English, and geography before lunch. History and PE after lunch. Today is _____.

2 Look at Activity 1 and write dialogues. Use *before* and *after*.

A: When do you have English?   A: When do you have PE?

B: On Mondays. After math.   B: On Wednesdays. Before lunch.

3 Write two sentences about your schedule.

1 On _____ I have _____ before _____.

2 _____ after _____.

School Subjects; *Before / After*

1 Look, read, and write sentences.

😀 like   😀 😀 love   😫 don't like

Tim

😀 Speaking English. Good at it.

😫 History. Not my favorite subject.

😀 😀 Listening to music.

Anna

😫 Learning math.

😀 Geography. Very good at it.

😀 😀 Studying history. Love my teacher, too.

1 _I like speaking English._
I'm good at it.

2 _____

3 _____
_____

4 _____
_____

5 _____
_____

6 _____
_____

2 Look and write sentences.

Jim   Claire   Mary   Sam   Lisa

1 _Jim doesn't like playing soccer._

2 _____

3 _____

4 _____

5 _____

3 Write about you.

I like _____.

I don't like _____.

1 Remember the song. Complete the words from the song. Use the letters in the circles to write a secret sentence.

There are lots of puzzles
To (1) f ⓘ ___ ___ the answers to.
They (2) h ___ ⓛ ___ us understand
What's false and what's true.

I love solving (3) ___ ◯ t ___ of problems,
And math is really cool.
Oh, yeah! I (4) ___ ___ ◯ e all the things
That we (5) ___ ◯ a ___ ___ at school!

I ⓛ ___ ___ ___ _____

2 Read Adam and Sarah's new verses. Write the words.

learning ~~reading~~ great working writing late day teachers

I love (1) __reading__ books in English.
I'm good at (2) _____ stories, hey!
I love (3) _____ about lots of things.
We learn at school all (4) _____.

I love (5) _____ on paper.
I think art's just (6) _____!
I really like my (7) _____.
That's why I'm never (8) _____!

3 Complete the school subjects. Then look and match.

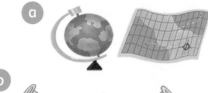

1 __E__ __n__ gl __i__ s h
2 h ___ s t ___ ___ y
3 m ___ t h
4 s ___ ___ ___ n c ___
5 g ___ ___ g r ___ p ___ y

4+2=6

1 Look and complete the sentences.

| do your homework   clean your shoes
wash your hands   ~~arrive at school~~
brush your teeth   get dressed | a meal   ~~nine o'clock~~   go and play
a meal   go to school   go to school |

1 You have to __arrive at school__ before __nine o'clock__.

2 You have to _____ after _____.

3 You have to _____ before _____.

4 You have to _____ before you can _____.

5 You have to _____ before you _____.

6 You have to _____ before you _____.

2 Write about you. Use *before*, *after*, *every day*, or *every week*.

At school

1 I have to _____.

2 I _____.

3 _____.

At home

1 I have to _____.

2 I _____.

3 _____.

1 Read the story *Getting Help* again. Put the lines in order.

- [ ] puzzles. He wants to keep the
- [ ] book. Ben and Lucy don't give it to him. Then
- [ ] code. They go to the librarian
- [1] Ben and Lucy can't read the book. It's in
- [ ] for help. He likes doing
- [ ] read the clues.
- [ ] they find the secret to the code. Now they can

2 Match the questions with the answers.

1 Can you help us, please?
2 What's the problem?
3 Can I keep the book?
4 What's going on? It's dark!
5 What's this here?
6 What about the code?

a No, sorry. We can't give it to you.
b Come on, Ben. We have to get out of here.
c Yes, of course.
d I don't understand the code yet. We have to follow those kids.
e We can't read this book. It's in code.
f It's the secret to the code.

3 Use the code on page 15 of the Student's Book. Write the words.

S e v e n

1 🎧 004 Listen and write the missing words. Then say with a friend.

Jim: What time is it, Fiona?

Fiona: It's half past three.

Jim: Really? _____ _____

_____ _____. Bye!

Fiona: Oh. Bye!

Sam: The car's too heavy.

Emma: Let's ask this man.

Sam: Good idea.

Emma: Excuse me. _____ _____

_____ _____, please?

2 🎧 005 Listen and write.

say	see		Ben		five	go	you	car
A	B	G	F	S				R
	C				Y			
							W	
	Z							

3 🎧 006 Listen, say, and check your answers.

1 🛡 **Read Oliver's story again. Complete the sentences.**

computer   ~~soccer and computer games~~
likes   day   numbers and dates   puzzle club

1 The children think Oliver is silly because he doesn't like
   soccer and computer games .

2 Oliver thinks stories are boring because they don't have

   _____.

3 Oliver can say what _____ it is when he looks
   at a date.

4 The children think Oliver is a _____.

5 Oliver wants to start a _____ at school.

6 Everyone _____ Oliver's idea.

2 **Read the story again. Check ✓ the correct sentences.**

1 The boys and girls think Oliver is different.   ☑

2 Oliver likes sitting under a tree and thinking.   ☐

3 Oliver likes listening to Ms. Sanders's stories.   ☐

4 Ms. Sanders writes the date of her birthday on the board.   ☐

5 The computer and Oliver say different days.   ☐

6 Mike wants to learn to do the same thing as Oliver.   ☐

3 🖐 🛡 **Read the story again and think. Color the circles green for *yes*
   or red for *no*.**

◯ Everyone is different.   ◯ Everyone is the same.

1 🎧 **007** Listen, color, and write. There is one example.

GEOMETRIC SHAPES

1 **Look at the pictures. Write the shapes.**

triangle   hexagon   pentagon

_____   _____   _____

2 **Circle the correct words. Then match.**

1 A hexagon has **six** / **five** sides.

2 A pentagon has **three** / **five** sides.

3 A triangle has **three** / **five** angles.

a  □

b  □

c  □

3 **Connect the blue dots in order with straight lines. Then answer the questions.**

1 How many different shapes are there now?

_____

2 What shapes are there?

_____

3 How many sides are there? _____

4 How many angles are there? _____

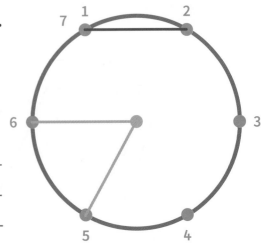

4 Read about tangrams. Write the answers to the questions.

A tangram is a Chinese puzzle with different shapes in a square. You can move the shapes to make different pictures. These shapes make a picture. What things do these shapes make? How many different shapes are there?

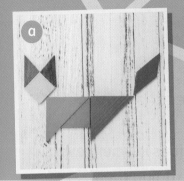 a
 b
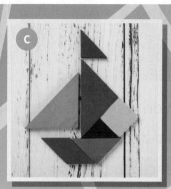 c
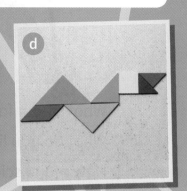 d

1 What things do these shapes make?
Write the words.

boat   snake   ~~cat~~   person

a __cat__   b _____   c _____   d _____

2 How many different shapes are there? _____

5 Color the tangram. Use the colors in the key.
What animal do you see?

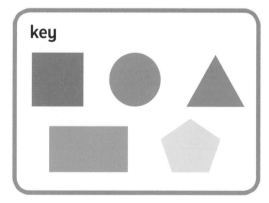

key

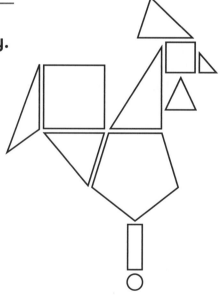

6 Make your own tangram. Draw and color it.
Then write about it.

This is a _____.
It has _____ shapes: _____
_____.
There are _____ sides and _____ angles.

1 Match the questions with the answers.

1 What's your favorite subject, Kate?

2 What do you like about it?

3 How many science classes do you have a week?

4 Do you have science today?

5 Do lots of students like science?

6 What's the favorite subject in your class?

a Three, but I'd like to have them every day.

b We do fun activities in science class, and I love doing them.

c No, not many children like it. They think it's difficult.

d For most of my classmates it's English. They love it.

e Science. I love it.

f Let me think. It's Wednesday. Yes, I have science after math.

2 Complete the report about the interview with Kate.

Kate's favorite subject is (1) **science** .

She loves (2)_____ .

Not many children (3)_____ .

Most children (4)_____ . On Wednesdays (5)_____

_____ .

3 Write about you and your school subjects.

My favorite subject is _____ .

_____

_____

_____

What do I know?

1 Look and draw lines to make sentences.

1

I

don't	likes	painting	the dog.
very	like	writing	books.
never	don't like	playing	pictures.

2

She

very	not likes	reading	the piano.
always	likes	watching	soccer.
doesn't	like	playing	TV.

3

You

have to	wash your	feet	before dinner.
has to	brush your	hands	after dinner.
have	wear you	face	before bed.

4

I

has to	wear	a uniform	in bed.
have to	wearing	a hat	at home.
has	not wear	a school bag	to school.

2 Read and think. Then write one more.

BIG QUESTION What kinds of puzzles are there?

There are different kinds of puzzles:
shape puzzles, number puzzles, _____

About me!

3 Read. Then write about you and draw.

I love playing with shapes.   _____

I like doing number puzzles.   _____

I don't like singing.   _____

1 Complete the crossword puzzle.

Down

Across

Crossword:
1 Down: v e g e t a b l e s
2 Across
3 Across
4 Across
5 Down
6 Down
7 Across
8 Across

2 Write words from Activity 1.

1 Can I have two bread __rolls_____, please?

2 Carrots and potatoes are _____.

3 It's usually yellow or white. _____

4 You wash your face with it, and you can drink it. _____

5 You drink this. It's sweet. _____

6 It's usually hot and you need a spoon to eat it. _____

spoon

3 Put the dialogue in order.

☐ Would you like a roll with cheese on it?

[1] I'm hungry.

☐ No, thanks. I don't like chicken.

☐ Yes, please. I'd love one.

☐ Would you like a roll with chicken on it?

1 Circle the correct words to complete the dialogue.

Kate: Guess what's in my lunch box!

Alice: There's (1) (some) / any bread. I think there's a roll.

Kate: That's right. What's on it?

Alice: Is there (2) some / any chicken?

Kate: No, there isn't. I don't like chicken.

Alice: OK, there isn't (3) some / any chicken. Is there (4) some / any cheese?

Kate: Cheese? Yes, there is. I love cheese.

Alice: Is there anything else in your lunch box?

Kate: Yes, there's (5) some / any water, too.

2 Complete the dialogues with *some* or *any*.

1 A: Is there __any__ water in that bottle?

   B: No, there isn't, but there is _____ orange juice.

2 A: Are there _____ onions on your roll?

   B: No, there aren't _____ onions.

3 A: Are there _____ carrots in the fridge?

   B: Yes, there are _____ carrots, but there aren't _____ apples.

4 A: Is there _____ chocolate, Mom?

   B: No, sorry, there isn't _____ chocolate. But there is _____ ice cream.

3 Draw your packed lunch and write.

There are some cheese and lettuce rolls.
There's an apple. There's some orange juice.

_____

_____

_____

_____

1 Write the words from the shopping list in the first verse. Make it rhyme. Write two more words for the second verse.

The Picnic Sandwich Song

Let's have a picnic!
It's going to be such fun.
We're going to go shopping,
For a picnic in the sun.

Are there any **(1)** _____?
Is there any **(2)** _____?
Yes, there are lots of
yummy things,
For me and my friend Pam!

Are there any **(3)** _____?
Is there any **(4)** _____?
Yes, there are lots of
yummy things,
These sandwiches look good!

2 Draw your own picnic sandwich. Write what's in it. Use *there is, there are, there isn't,* and *there aren't.*

In my picnic sandwich, there is some
cheese. There isn't any chocolate.
_____
_____
_____
_____
_____
_____
_____

1 Put the words in order. Then read and write *Ava, Lilly,* or *Olivia.*

_____   Ava   _____

1 Liam:	we / put / some / peas and carrots / our / soup / in / should / ?
	_____
Ava:	Peas are OK, but I don't want any carrots. Should we put in some tomatoes?
Liam:	OK.

2 Gabriel:	you / like / some / fish soup / would / ?
	_____
Lilly:	Sorry, no. I don't like fish. How about potato soup?
Gabriel:	Good idea! Should we put some onions in it, too?
Lilly:	Yes.

3 Aidan:	I'd / some / soup / like / vegetable / .
	_____
Olivia:	OK.
Aidan:	Should we put carrots and peas in it?
Olivia:	I'm not sure. How about tomatoes?
Aidan:	Yummy!

2 Complete the dialogues with your own ideas.

1 A: Should we make some vegetable soup?

  B: Good idea. Should we put in some _____, too?

  A: Yes.

2 A: Should we _____ in the soup?

  B: I'm not sure. How about _____?

  A: Yummy!

3 A: _____ ?

  B: Yes. Let's put some _____ in it, too.

  A: Good idea.

1 **Read the story *The Golden Apple* again. Then circle the correct words.**

1 A (snake) / **dog** / **bee** bites Buster.

2 Ben and Lucy want to go to the **school** / **library** / **town**.

3 An old man tells them to go to the **basement** / **waterfall** / **town** at the top of the mountain.

4 Only the golden **tomato** / **orange** / **apple** can help Buster.

5 Horax and Zelda want to **take** / **eat** / **cook** the apple, too.

6 The children write **an apple** / **the letter *I*** / **an idea** in the book.

2 **Write more things for Ben to say. Use the words from the box or your own ideas.**

call the police   make some tea   take him to the vet   sing him a song   get help

Should we _____?

Let's _____.

We can _____.

Do you want to _____?

Let's take him to the town.

3 Read the story. What can we learn from it? Draw 😃 or 😣.

◯ When things don't work, stop trying.

◯ When things don't work, tell yourself, "I can do it!"

Helen Keller is born in 1880 in Alabama, U.S.A. When she is two years old, she has a terrible illness. She can't see and can't hear. Her parents are very sad. They can't speak with Helen any more.

The doctors can't help Helen. In 1887, her parents find her a teacher, Anne Sullivan. She tries to teach Helen the alphabet. This is very difficult for Helen because she can't see or hear.

Helen Keller

One day, Anne Sullivan is using her finger to write "water" on Helen's hand. She puts Helen's other hand in a bowl of water. Suddenly Helen understands. On that day, she learns 30 words.

The little girl is very smart. She soon learns how to write, and she even learns to speak. Many of the things she wants to learn are very difficult, but she never gives up. Later, she goes to college and spends her life helping other people.

1 🎧 008 Listen and write the missing words. Then say with a friend.

1

Kim: _____ _____ _____, Daniel?

Daniel: It's my head. It hurts.

Kim: Should I get you some medicine?

Daniel: No, it's OK. It's not too bad.

Tom: What are you doing, Mary?

Mary: I want this book. It's really good.

Tom: Can I help you?

Mary: No, thanks. _____ _____
_____ _____ _____.

2 🎧 009 Listen, point, and say. Write the words.

> I spy with my little eye something beginning with …

bike _____

1 Read about school lunches around the world. Check ☑ your favorite lunch. Complete the sentence to say why.

Michelle ☐

> I live in France. School lunch starts at one o'clock. I usually have rice, fish, some bread, and a small salad. I sometimes have a banana, too.

> We have lunch at half past one in Spain. We usually have vegetable soup, meat, salad, some bread, and fruit. We usually have a piece of cake, too.

Pablo ☐

Evelina ☐

> In Greece, we go home for lunch at half past two. We have a big lunch with meat or fish and a big salad. We also have vegetables. We have fruit after lunch.

My favorite lunch is _____'s lunch because _____

_____ .

2 🛡 Look at Activity 1 again. Answer the questions.

Who has:

1 fish for lunch?   <u>Michelle and Evelina</u>   4 some cake?   _____

2 lunch at home?   _____   5 a big lunch?   _____

3 soup for lunch?   _____   6 rice and fish?   _____

3 Write about your lunch. Then draw.

I have lunch at _____ .

I usually have _____

_____ .

Sometimes I have _____ .

1 🎧 **010** Listen and check ✓ the correct answer.

Dinner Around the World

1 For dinner, Teresa's family eats
A ☐ salad and fish. B ✓ salad, vegetables, and meat.
C ☐ salad, vegetables, and fish.

2 In Chuck's family, nobody has lunch
A ☐ at home. B ☐ at work. C ☐ at school.

3 Chuck and his family talk about
A ☐ the weekend. B ☐ the day. C ☐ TV.

4 On the weekend, Carlos has dinner at
A ☐ eight o'clock. B ☐ nine o'clock. C ☐ ten o'clock.

5 Carlos likes eating
A ☐ beans and chips. B ☐ beans and rice. C ☐ carrots and rice.

2 🛡 **Remember Activity 1. Write *Carlos*, *Chuck*, or *Teresa*.**

_____ _____ _____

3 **Complete the paragraph about you.**

I'm from _____. We usually start dinner at _____.
My favorite dinner is _____.

Edible Plants

1 Look and write the edible plant part in each picture.

stems
seeds
leaves
fruit
~~roots~~

beets: **roots**

green onion: _____

spinach: _____

sesame seeds: _____

pears: _____

2 Read and circle the correct words.

To: penny@megamail.com   Subject: Dinner!

Dear Penny,

Tonight, we're having a nice dinner. There's a delicious salad with spinach and lettuce
(1) stems /(leaves) There's also a delicious soup with asparagus (2) **roots / stems**.
We have some chicken with pumpkin (3) **seeds / leaves**. We also have a salad with
(4) **roots / fruit**: carrots and beets. There's also a glass of (5) **fruit / stem** juice for me
with strawberries and mango – my favorite!

What's for dinner at your home?

Mark

3 Think of a plant part. What food comes from it? Write about it.

___**Leaves**___ are part of a plant. ___**Lettuce**___ comes from this part.

4 Write names of plants and plant parts we can use to make these things.

soup: _stems_ , _____

juice: _____ , _____

salad: _____ , _____

5 Look at the animals. Write the food they eat. You can use some words more than once.

seeds   stems   fruit   roots   leaves

fruit,

6 Read and complete the menu with your own ideas. Add one more plant part.

LUNCH MENU

Green salad with _____ leaves.

Vegetable soup with _____ and _____ roots.

Rice with _____ .

Fruit juice with _____ and _____ .

_____ .

1 🎧 **011** **Put the dialogue in order. Then listen and check.**

☐ A: OK, so that's pizza with cheese, onions, peppers, and tomatoes.

☐ A: Let me see. Yes, we have peppers.

☐ A: Sorry, we don't have any mushrooms.

1 A: Hello. Can I help you?

☐ B: That's great. Can I have some tomatoes, too?

☐ B: I'd like a pizza with cheese, mushrooms, and onions, please.

☐ B: No mushrooms? Do you have any peppers?

2 🛡 **Look and write a dialogue. Use language from Activity 1.**

Assistant: <u>Hello! Can I help you?</u>

Boy: _____

_____

_____

_____

_____

What do I know?

1 Color the bricks to make sentences. Write in the missing words.

1	Is <u>there</u>	make some vegetable	in the fridge.
2	There aren't	_____ cheese	a salad?
3	_____ we	about _____	_____ lemonade.
4	How	_____ oranges	soup?
5	Let's make	a bottle	in my sandwich?

2  Read and think. Then write three more.

BIG QUESTION   What's good to eat?

It's good to eat different food: chicken, peas, roots,

_____ , _____ , _____

About me!

3 Read. Then write about you and draw.

My favorite dinner is chicken, peas,
and fries. I have dinner at 7 o'clock.
I don't like fish and rice.

_____

_____

_____

_____

_____

_____

_____

_____

3 Daily Tasks

1 **Match the words.**

1 clean   a the shopping
2 cook   b up
3 take   c the floor
4 dry   d the dishes
5 sweep   e the dog
6 do   f the dog for a walk
7 do   g dinner
8 feed   h the dishes

2 **Look and write the actions.**

1 d r y t h e
  d i s h e s

2 c _ _ _ _
  d _ _ _ _ _ _

3 s _ _ _ _ _ _ t _ _ _
  f _ _ _ _ _

4 d _ t _ _ _
  s _ _ _ _ _ _ _ _

5 d _ _ _ _ _ _
  d _ _ _ _ _ _ _

6 t _ _ _ _ t _ _
  d _ _ _ f _ _ _
  a w _ _ _ _

7 c _ _ _ _ _
  u _ _

8 f _ _ _ _
  t _ _ _ d _ _ _

3 **Write about you.**

I like taking the dog for a walk. I don't like cleaning up.

_____

1

🎧 012 **Listen and check ☑ the correct box.**

1 ☐ ☑

2 ☐ ☐

3 ☐ ☐

4 ☐ ☐

5 ☐ ☐

6 ☐ ☐

2

What time do you do these things? Write sentences with the words from the box.

go to school   do my homework   have breakfast   go to bed   ~~get up~~

1 I get up at _____.

2 _____.

3 _____.

4 _____.

5 _____.

1  Remember the song and match. Read the song again to check.

a half past three

b half past ten

c half past nine

d quarter to three

e nine o'clock

2 Read the song again. Complete the sentences about the pilot.

is in her spaceship   is at her door   is on the moon   ~~gets up~~   is back home   works

1 She _gets up_ at quarter to three.

2 She _____ at nine o'clock.

3 She _____ at half past nine.

4 She _____ at half past ten.

5 She _____ at half past three.

6 She _____ at night.

3 Imagine you are the pilot of a spaceship. Write your own verse and draw.

○ I'm in my spaceship. It's _____.

○ I'm the pilot and _____.

○ It's _____, I'm on the moon.

○ _____. _____.

1 Look at the table and read. Write *t* (true) or *f* (false).

What we do on Saturdays.	🎾	🎟️ CINEMA TICKET	📱 555-3421	📚
Rob	✓✓✓	✓	✗	✓
Gillian	✓✓	✓✓✓	✓✓	✗

✓✓✓ = always ✓✓ = usually ✓ = sometimes ✗ = never

1 Rob sometimes goes to the movies on Saturdays. `t`

2 Gillian usually calls her friends on Saturdays. ☐

3 Rob always does his homework on Saturdays. ☐

4 Gillian sometimes plays tennis on Saturdays. ☐

5 Rob never calls his friends on Saturdays. ☐

2 Write four more true sentences about Rob and Gillian.

_____

_____

_____

_____

3 Complete the sentences about you.
Use the words from the box.

I always eat pizza on Fridays.

always   usually   sometimes   never

1 I _____ eat pizza on Fridays.

2 I _____ watch TV on Saturdays.

3 I _____ get up before seven o'clock.

4 I _____ walk to school.

5 I _____ go swimming on the weekend.

Me too!

1 Read the story *Cleaning Up* again. Answer the questions.

1 Why does Ben want to look for the letter in the morning?   <u>Because he's tired.</u>

2 What time do Horax and Zelda go home?   _____

3 Where does Ben look for the letter first?   _____

4 Where does Lucy look for the letter first?   _____

5 Where does Lucy find the letter?   _____

6 What is the second letter?   _____

2 Check ✓ the best answer.

1 Look at pictures 1 and 3. What's the same about Ben and Zelda?

a ☐ They are angry.   b ☐ They are tired.   c ☐ They are hungry.

2 Look at picture 8. What's the same about Lucy and Ben?

a ☐ They are sad.   b ☐ They are angry.   c ☐ They are excited.

3 Look at pictures 6 and 8. What's different about Lucy?

a ☐ First she is happy, then she is unhappy.

b ☐ First she is unhappy, then she is happy.

c ☐ First she is scared, then she is not tired.

1 🎧 **013** **Listen and write the missing words. Then say with a friend.**

Dad: Close your eyes, Molly.

Molly: Why?

Dad: _____ _____ _____
_____ _____ _____.

Molly: What is it?

Dad: OK. Open them.

Molly: Dad! You're the best!

Mom: _____ _____ _____!

Dan: What's the problem, Mom?

Mom: Your room! Look at it! I want it clean.

Dan: But I cleaned it last week, Mom.

2 **Look and write *v*, *f*, or *ff*.**

1 **f** our   2 __egetables   3 __ruit   4 hea __y

5 __i__teen   6 water__all   7 se__enteen   8 di___icult

3 🎧 **014** **Listen and say.**

1 Read the shoemaker's story again. Check ✓ the correct sentences.

1 The shoemaker works a lot of hours. ✓

2 The shoemaker works hard but has little money. ☐

3 Every morning, he finds new shoes on the table. ☐

4 The elves work after 5 o'clock in the morning. ☐

5 The shoemaker makes nice clothes for the elves to thank them. ☐

6 The elves still make shoes for the shoemaker. ☐

2 Read the story again. Complete the summary with the words from the box.

every   doesn't   old   leather   happy   ~~shoemaker~~   next

There is a (1) __shoemaker__ who works very hard. One night, he cuts some (2) _____ and leaves it on the kitchen table. In the morning, there are ten pairs of beautiful shoes. The (3) _____ morning there are twenty pairs of beautiful shoes. Every night, he leaves leather on the table, and (4) _____ morning there are beautiful new shoes. Soon, everyone in the town wants more shoes from the shoemaker. But the shoemaker (5) _____ know who makes the shoes. One night he hides under a table and sees five elves making shoes. They are wearing (6) _____ clothes. The shoemaker makes nice clothes for the elves. The elves take the clothes, but they don't come back to make new shoes. The shoemaker doesn't mind because he wants the elves to be (7) _____.

3 Read the story again and think. Color the circles green for *yes* or red for *no*.

◯ Be kind to others.   ◯ Don't think about others.

1 **Look at the pictures and write the words.**

> ~~Mom very tired~~   Patty and Jack help Mom   Patty and Jack do the dishes
> Mom needs help   Mom takes a nap   Patty and Jack make lunch
> Patty, Jack, and Mom have a nice lunch   ~~house is messy~~   dog is hungry

house is messy, Mom very tired

_____

_____   _____

_____   _____

2 **Write the story. Use the words from Activity 1 to help you.**

Jack and Patty's mom is tired because the house is messy.

_____

_____

JOBS AT *Night*

1 🛡 **Look at these jobs. Write *d* (day only) or *b* (both day and night).**

teacher

security guard

ambulance driver

salesclerk

nurse

<u>d</u> ___ ___ ___ ___

2 **Read and write the jobs.** [janitor   police officer   pilot]

1
My dad works during the day and at night. He flies a plane and takes people to different countries. He usually gets tired, and his job is very hard. I don't like his job because he doesn't see us every day.

_____

2
My mom works very hard. Sometimes she leaves home at 8 o'clock in the evening and comes back early in the morning. Her job can be dangerous, but she loves keeping people safe. I want to be like my mom when I grow up.

_____

3
My sister is always tired after work. She cleans big offices and works late at night. She never comes home before 1 o'clock in the morning. She doesn't like her job because it's difficult.

_____

3 🛡 **Complete the sentences with your own ideas.**

I think working at night is _____.

I think working in the day is _____.

4 **Read Pedro's diary and match.**

Pedro

I always leave home at quarter past seven every evening before my family has dinner. I start work at eight o'clock. I always have dinner at half past eleven. Work is always very busy, and sometimes it is very difficult. I go home at five o'clock in the morning, and I always go to bed. I get up at three o'clock and have a small breakfast. When my children come home, I help them with their homework. Then we take our dog for a walk. I have lunch at quarter past six – a sandwich and some fruit. I think my job is difficult, but I love helping sick people.

1 quarter past seven   a go home
2 eight o'clock   b have lunch
3 half past eleven   c leave home
4 five o'clock in the morning d have dinner
5 quarter past six   e start work

5 **Circle the correct words.**

1 Pedro **always** / **never** has dinner with his family.
2 He **never** / **always** starts work at eight o'clock.
3 His work is **always** / **sometimes** very difficult.
4 He **never** / **always** goes to bed after work.
5 He **never** / **always** has lunch.

6 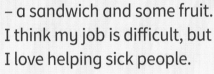 **Imagine you work at night. Complete the sentences about your job.**

I'm a _____ .

I start work at _____ .

I sometimes have lunch at _____ .

I never _____ .

I always _____ .

I think my job is _____ .

1 Match the questions with the answers.

1 What housework do you do, Stuart?

2 Do you sometimes do the dishes?

3 What's your favorite job?

4 Do you like cooking?

5 What's your least favorite job?

6 Do you get money for doing housework?

a It's OK.

b I clean my room, and I walk the dog every day. I cook breakfast on the weekend.

c Cleaning my room. I hate doing that.

d No, but my dad pays me $5 when I help in the yard.

e No, I don't. Mom doesn't want me to break her plates.

f Walking the dog. I love it.

2 Read about Stuart. Underline the mistakes. Then write the correct sentences.

Stuart has to clean his bedroom and <u>feed</u> the dog every day. On the weekend, he cooks dinner. He doesn't have to do the dishes. His mom doesn't want him to break her plates! His favorite job is cooking. He loves doing that. He doesn't like cleaning his room. That's his least favorite job. He doesn't get paid for doing housework, but his mom gives him $5 when he does the dishes.

Stuart has to walk the dog every day.

_____

_____

_____

_____

3 Write about how you help at home.

I have to make my bed every day.

I have to do the dishes on Fridays.

1 What do I know? Look and draw lines to make sentences.

1 I

get home	after dinner	at	quarter to two.
have breakfast	before lunch	in	four o'clock.
go to bed	from school	on	half past three.

2 She

has breakfast	by	quarter to	six.
gets dressed	in	quarter past	seven.
goes to school	at	half past	eight.

3 You

plays always	tennis	after	school.
always plays	soccer	before	dinner.
always play	the piano	on	breakfast.

4 He

never	do homework	on	Mondays.
sometimes	does homework	in	Wednesdays.
always	doing homework	out	Sundays.

2 Read, think, and circle. Then write one more pair.

BIG QUESTION What's it like to work at night?

Work at night can be: fun / boring, busy / quiet, _____

About me! 3 Read. Then write about you and draw.

I clean my room at half past six. I like
cleaning my room. I sometimes do the
dishes. I don't dry the dishes. _____

_____

_____

4 Around Town

1 Look at the letters on the signs. Write the words.

rafi

ankb

kemart

wetor

laybrri

bsu tsaiont

rkgpnai tol

soprst etcren

1 fair
2 _____
3 _____
4 _____
5 _____
6 _____
7 _____
8 _____

2 Look and write the places.

library

t_____

p_____ l_____

m_____

b_____

s_____ c_____

3 What places are there where you live? Complete the sentence.

Where I live, there is a _____.

1 **Look and write. Use the words from the box.**   below above ~~close to~~ across from

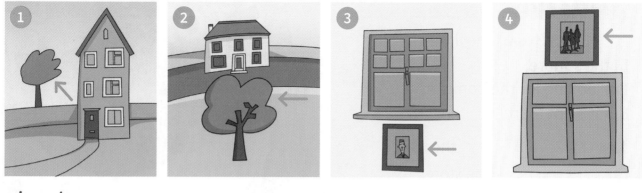

close to _____   _____   _____   _____

2 **Look at the picture. Complete the sentences.**

1 The movie theater is **across from** the library.

2 The tower is _____ the movie theater.

3 The park is _____ the school.

4 The boat is _____ the bridge.

5 The sports center is _____ the movie theater and the café.

6 The castle is _____ the sports center.

3 **Write two sentences about places where you live.**

The _____ is _____ .

The _____ is _____ .

1 Read the song again. Then complete.

(1) **Across from** the library,
In the square,
I'm looking for the bank,
But it's not there.

Just (2) _____ the tower,
(3) _____ the store,
My map says there's a café,
But there is not.

(4) _____ the station,
In the street,
There's a place
Where people always meet.

2 Complete the song with your own ideas and then draw.

Across from the _____,
In the _____,
I'm looking for the _____,
But it's not there.

Just below the _____,
Close to the _____,
My map says there's a _____,
But there is not.

In front of the _____,
In the _____,
There's a place
Where people always meet.

1 **Put the words in order.**

1 friends / I'm / going / to / meet / to / town / my / the

   <u>I'm going to the town to meet my friends.</u>

2 the / I'm / going / to / to / some / supermarket / milk / buy

   _____

3 house / I'm / to / my / to / play / friend's / computer games / going

   _____

4 to / going / to / the / I'm / ride / park / bike / my

   _____

2 **Look, read, and write.** ~~to buy~~   to listen to   to play   to get

William: Where are you going, Harry? To the park?

Harry: No, I'm not. I'm going to the supermarket (1) <u>to buy</u> some apples.

Emma: Oh, Olivia. Where are you going?

Olivia: I'm going to a friend's house (2) _____ music.

Linda: Hi, Sue. Let's go to the park.

Sue: Sorry, Linda. I'm going to the library (3) _____ a book.

John: Hi, Jeff. Where are you going?

Jeff: I'm going to the park (4) _____ tennis.

3 **Complete the sentences. Use your own ideas.**

I'm going to the supermarket to _____.

I'm going to the park to _____.

I'm going to my friend's house to _____.

Where are you going?

1 Read the story *Up High* again. Write the words.

1 Lucy and Ben are going to the tower to get the next __letter__.

2 Lucy and Ben have their _____ with them.

3 "Look, the tower's over there, _____ the school."

4 "Lucy! Where are you _____?"

5 Lucy and Ben are really _____ on the Pirate Ship.

close to
going
high
~~letter~~
dog

2 Put the lines in order.

[ ] Then Lucy doesn't go to the tower. She goes to the fair.

[1] Ben and Lucy know that the tower is close to the market.

[ ] Ben wants to go to the fair. Lucy says, "We're going to the tower."

[ ] Ben and Lucy go on the Pirate Ship. They are above the tower.

[ ] Horax and Zelda are in the tower. It's the wrong place.

3 Read the story below. What can we learn from it? Draw 😃 or 😖.

( ) It's often good to try out new ideas.   ( ) Never listen to others.

Emma: Tomorrow is Dad's birthday. What can we give him?

Tom: We always buy a CD for him. He loves music.

Emma: What about something different?

Tom: Do you have an idea?

Emma: Yes, I do. Let's buy a T-shirt. There's a store in the town. They can print a photo on the T-shirt.

Tom: Great idea. And we can print "Dad, we love you!" on it, too.

Emma: Yes, let's do that.

The next day …

Emma/Tom: Happy birthday, Dad!

Dad: What a wonderful present! Thank you.

Dad, we love you!

1 🎧 015 **Listen and write the missing words. Then say with a friend.**

Dan: I want to stay.	**Sue:** An owl!
Mom: Sorry. _____ _____ _____ _____.	**Aaron:** Where? I can't see anything.
Dan: It's not fair.	**Sue:** _____, _____ _____ _____. Above your head.
Mom: We have to go home now.	**Aaron:** Oh, yeah. Wow! It's beautiful.

2 🎧 016 **Listen and write.**

1 **r a i n** 2 __ __ __ 3 __ __ __ __ __ 4 __ __ __

5 __ __ __ __ 6 __ __ __ 7 __ __ __ __

3 🎧 017 **Listen and say.**

🎧 018 **Listen and draw lines. There is one example.**

Hannah   Mike   Christine

Olivia   Ben   William

1 **Read the text and choose the best answer.**

Example

Paul: I think we're lost.

Daisy: A There's a bus stop across from the bank.

   B I think it's a parking lot.

   Ⓒ Let's look at the map.

Questions

1 Paul: Look! Can you see the museum?

  Daisy: A Yes, it's close to the market.

    B It's a big place.

    C There's a café.

2 Paul: OK. Where are we going now?

  Daisy: A The tower is over there.

    B It's above the window.

    C We're going to the library.

3 Paul: Why are we going there?

  Daisy: A To borrow a book about Egypt.

    B We're going on Sunday.

    C It's a castle.

4 Paul: I'm a little hungry.

  Daisy: A We can go to the sports center.

    B We can buy a sandwich at the supermarket.

    C Let's go to the fair.

5 Paul: Oh, no! I don't have any money!

  Daisy: A OK. Let's go to the bank.

    B The library isn't open now.

    C There's a park across from the market.

6 Paul: What a long day. Where can we get some rest?

  Daisy: A Yes, let's get a salad.

    B No, it's not close to the market.

    C Let's go to the park and sit under a tree.

TALL BUILDINGS

1 **Read and write the words.**

lighthouse   skyscraper   airport tower   ~~clock tower~~

1

This is my favorite building in our town. It's very tall and old. I listen to the bells that ring every hour so that I know what time it is.

It's a/an __clock tower__ .

2

My dad's job is tiring because he has to climb many stairs. He goes to the top of the tower every day and cleans a big light. He makes sure it always works because it keeps boats safe.

It's a/an _____ .

3

Mom checks traffic in the sky so that airplanes don't have accidents. She uses computers to help her. These computers show her where airplanes are in the sky.

It's a/an _____ .

4

We always go to the top of this building so that we can see the city below us. There's a big café and a restaurant there, too. I love seeing the airplanes fly by, and sometimes the clouds are so close that you think you are flying in them.

It's a/an _____ .

2 **Which tall buildings do you want to visit? Why? Write sentences.**

I want to visit a clock tower so that I can see how big the clock in it is.

I want to visit a _____ .

_____

3 **Look and match.**

The Eiffel Tower

The Empire State Building

The Amazon Tall Tower Observatory

a This is a tower in the rainforest. Scientists use it to study the rainforest and weather. It is 325 meters tall. ☐

b This tower is in Paris, and many people climb it so that they can see the city below. It is a very famous tower, and many tourists visit it. ☐

c This building has many offices in it, and more than 20,000 people work in it. There is also a special area for people to visit so that they can see New York below. ☐

4 **Read and check ✓.**

1 The Eiffel Tower is tall so that
- ☐ people can see the city.
- ☐ people can finish building it.

2 The Empire State Building is tall so that
- ☐ lots of people can work there.
- ☐ tourists can see 20,000 people.

3 The Amazon Tall Tower Observatory is tall so that
- ☐ animals can climb it.
- ☐ scientists can see the rainforest.

5 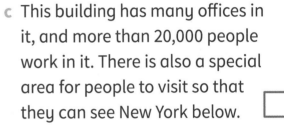 **Think of a famous tall building. Why is it tall? Write two sentences. Then draw.**

The _____ is tall so that _____.

People use it _____.

1 🎧 **019** **Put the dialogue in order. Then listen and check.**

☐ **B:** Yes, of course.

☐ **B:** It's next to the bank.

☐ **A:** Thank you. That's very kind.

☐ **B:** The bus station is across from the library.

1 **A:** Excuse me. Can you help me, please?

☐ **A:** Where's the bus station?

☐ **B:** You're welcome!

☐ **A:** OK. And where's the library?

2 🛡 **Look and write a dialogue. Use language from Activity 1.**

Woman: <u>Excuse me. Can you help me, please?</u>

Girl: _____

_____

_____

_____

_____

_____

1 **What do I know?** Color the bricks to make sentences. Write in the missing words.

1	I'm going	café to get	to get a book.
2	We're going to	to the sports center to	park.
3	He's _____ to the	the _____	_____ bus station.
4	The museum _____	across from the	a sandwich.
5	The café	is close to	_play_ tennis.

2 Read and think. Then write two more.   **BIG QUESTION** **What do we find in towns?**

In a town we can find: a tower, a library, a parking lot,
_____, and _____ .

3 **About me!** Read. Then write about your town and draw.

There's a museum, a market,
and a library where I live.
There isn't a bank.

_____
_____
_____

1 Complete the words. Then look and match.

1 <u>s e a h o r s e</u>
2 d __ __ p __ __ __ __
3 t __ __ t __ __ __
4 o __ __ __ p __ __ __
5 s __ __ __ __
6 s __ __ __ __ f __ __ __
7 s __ __ __ l
8 a __ __ __ __ o __

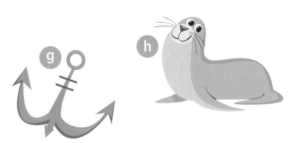

2 Read and write words from Activity 1.

1 It has a hard shell. <u>turtle</u>
2 It has eight arms. _____

3 A boat has one of these. _____
4 An animal lives inside this. _____

3 Read and write the words from the box.

> follow   love   sure   smart   worry   ~~anywhere~~

Dad: Where's our boat? I can't see it (1) <u>anywhere</u>.

Angela: I don't know. Wow! Look, a dolphin! I (2) _____ dolphins!

Dad: Yes, they are beautiful … and very (3) _____. Let's (4) _____ it!

Angela: Are you (5) _____?

Dad: Yes. Don't (6) _____. I think the dolphin is taking care of us.

1 Read and complete with *was, wasn't, were,* or *weren't*.

The Golden Toad

Many years ago, there **(1)** __were__ golden toads in
Costa Rica. There **(2)** _____ many pools for them.
It **(3)** _____ very hot in 1987, and there **(4)** _____
any water in the pools. There **(5)** _____ no more
golden toads.

The T-Rex

Millions of years ago there **(6)** _____ dinosaurs.
Most dinosaurs **(7)** _____ very big. There **(8)**_____
a change in the climate, and it **(9)** _____ very cold.
There **(10)** _____ food for the dinosaurs. There
(11) _____ any more dinosaurs.

2 Look and complete the sentences.

A Long Time Ago

Now

1 A long time ago, there __was a house behind the swimming pool__ .

2 A long time ago, there _____ .

3 A long time _____ .

4 A long _____ .

5 A _____ .

6 _____ .

1 🎧 020 🛡 **Remember the song and complete the sentences.**
Then listen and check.

starfish ~~octopus~~ turtle Crocorox

1 The _octopus_ was sad.

2 The _____ was bad.

3 The _____ hid inside its shell.

4 The _____ were all very scared.

2 **Read and complete the sentences.**

1 Its face was pretty. No, _it wasn't_ .
  It _was ugly_ .

2 Its eyes were small. Yes, _____ .

3 Its teeth were short. No, _____ .
  They _____ .

4 Its face was square. Yes, _____ .

5 There were scales on its head. Yes, _____ .

3 🛡 **Draw your own scary ocean animal. Complete the verse about it.**
Then write about the other ocean animals.

Its face _____ .

Its eyes _____ .

Its teeth _____ .

The dolphins were _____ .

The seals were _____ .

_____ .

1 **Look and write questions or answers.**

1 Was Max at the beach at six o'clock?   Yes, he was.

2 _____   No, she wasn't.

3 Were George and Harry in the park at quarter to five? _____

4 _____   Yes, they were.

5 Was Lucas in the square at half past four? _____

2 **Put the words in order to make questions. Then complete the answers.**

1 the / was / heavy / bag / ?

Was the bag heavy? _____   Yes, it was.

2 with / were / you / John / ?

_____   No, _____.

3 helping / was / her grandmother / in the yard / Emma / ?

_____   No, _____.

4 fish / there / in the river / lots / of / were / ?

_____   Yes, _____.

3 **Complete the question. Then answer for you.**

Where _____ you at six o'clock yesterday?

I _____.

1 Read the story *The Trap* again. Write *t* (true) or *f* (false).

1 The next letter is in the giant shell. `f`

2 Lucy can't get her arm out of the giant shell. ☐

3 The shark was in Horax's cage. ☐

4 The shark likes Horax and Zelda. ☐

5 The octopus can't help the children. ☐

6 The fish make the letter S. ☐

2 Put the lines in order.

☐ Finally, the children look at the fish and see the letter S.

☐ They see Horax and Zelda and the shark.

`1` First, Lucy and Ben dive down to a giant shell.

☐ Ben can't see a letter in the shell.

☐ The octopus helps Ben get his arm out.

☐ Zelda says, "I don't think the shark is very happy with us."

☐ The shark doesn't get the children. It follows Horax and Zelda.

☐ Then Ben can't get his arm out of the shell.

3 Which pictures are these from the story? Look and write the picture number.

1 🎧 021 **Listen and write the missing words. Then say with a friend.**

John: Why is that dog barking?

Sue: _____ _____
_____ _____.

John: Me? Don't be silly! All dogs like me.

Sue: Well, I'm not sure about this one.

Ingrid: What's the matter, Oliver?

Oliver: It's this box. _____
_____ _____ _____.

Ingrid: Here, let me try. There you go.
It was easy.

Oliver: Wow! You're strong.

2 **Look and write s, sh, or c.**

1 **sh** ell 2 ___ ark 3 o ___ ean 4 ___ ip 5 ___ wim

6 fi ___ 7 octopu ___ 8 ___ eahor ___ e 9 ___ tarfi ___ 10 Lu ___ y

3 🎧 022 **Listen and say.**

1   **Listen to Kylie's story again and write.**

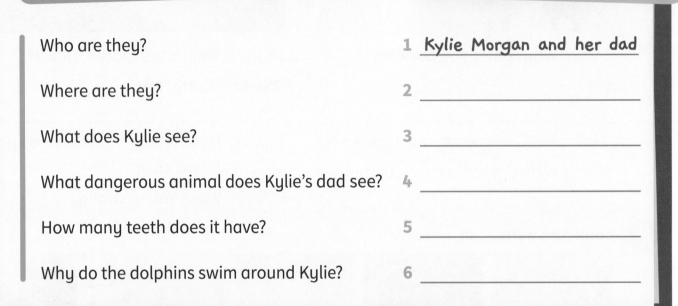

FACT SHEET

Who are they?	1	Kylie Morgan and her dad
Where are they?	2	
What does Kylie see?	3	
What dangerous animal does Kylie's dad see?	4	
How many teeth does it have?	5	
Why do the dolphins swim around Kylie?	6	

2 **Write *t* (true) or *f* (false).**

1 The dolphins hit their tails on the water to scare the sharks. ☐ t

2 The dolphins get close to Kylie to protect her. ☐

3 The white shark plays with the dolphins. ☐

4 Sharks aren't dangerous animals. ☐

5 The dolphins save Kylie from the shark. ☐

3 **Read the story again and think. Color the circles green for *yes* or red for *no*.**

○ You should always be scared in the ocean.

○ You should stay calm and think when in danger.

1 Look at the pictures and write the words.

> takes her to the beach   ~~Elena and her dad are fishing~~   dolphin comes
> falls into the ocean   can't swim   dad feeds dolphin   ~~happy~~

Elena and her dad
are fishing, happy

2 Write the story. Use the words from Activity 1 to help you.

Elena and her dad are fishing ...

People and the Ocean

1 Look and match the pictures to the happy or sad faces. Then complete the sentences.

Pictures **2** _____, _____, and _____ make me feel happy because
<u>the animals are safe,</u> _____

Pictures _____, _____, and _____ make me feel angry because

_____

2 Look at the pictures of Paul in 1990 and today. Complete the sentences.

In 1990 …
… the beach (1) <u>was</u> clean.
… people (2) _____ in the ocean.
… there (3) _____ fish and dolphins in the ocean, too.
… Paul (4) _____ happy.

Today …
… the beach (5) _____ clean.
… there (6) _____ trash on the beach.
… there (7) _____ any fish in the ocean.
… Paul (8) _____ happy.

3 Write the words or phrases in the correct column.
Then add one more word or phrase to each column.

~~world getting hotter~~   plastic bags   floods
poles melting   big boats   ocean creatures eat plastic

Climate Change	Pollution
world getting hotter	

4 Circle the correct words.

1 Ocean plants give us (oxygen) / pollution.

2 Cities by the ocean are in danger because there is **more** / **less** water in the ocean.

3 **Hot** / **Cold** water is bad for coral.

4 Fish are losing their homes because coral **is turning white** / **has beautiful colors**.

5 Ocean creatures die because **they** / **we** eat plastic.

6 Big boats are **good** / **bad** for our oceans.

5 Think and write.

To protect our environment, I can:

_____
_____
_____
_____
_____
_____
_____
_____

1 Match the questions with the answers.

1 Where were you on Saturday afternoon, Charlotte?

2 Who was with you?

3 Was the movie good?

4 What was it about?

5 Were you at Ruby's birthday party on Saturday evening?

6 Why not?

a Yes, it was.

b I was at the movies.

c No, I wasn't.

d I was too tired.

e It was about a girl and a boy. They become best friends.

f My dad.

2 Read about Charlotte. Underline the mistakes. Then write the correct sentences.

On Saturday <u>morning</u>, Charlotte was at the movies. She was with her mom. The movie wasn't very good. It was about two girls. They become best friends. In the evening Charlotte was at Ruby's birthday party.

On Saturday afternoon, Charlotte was at the movies.

_____

_____

_____

_____

3 Write about your Saturday afternoon.

On Saturday afternoon, I was at the park. I was with my friends.

What do I know?

1 Look and draw lines to make sentences.

1

There

was	many seahorses	at	the ocean.
were	many octopuses	in	the yard.
weren't	many starfish	on	the bath.

2

The

owl	was	in	the school.
dolphin	were	next to	the ocean.
lion	weren't	across from	the beach.

3

Where

was	it	at	four o'clock?
am	she	in	half past three?
are	they	by	quarter to four?

4

Where

are	my bag?	Under	the net.
were	my bags?	On	the table.
was	my table?	Next	to the sofa.

2 Read and think. Then write two more.

BIG QUESTION What's in the ocean?

In the ocean, there are many animals: sharks, dolphins, _____ , _____

About me!

3 Read. Then write about you and draw.

I was at the beach on Saturday. _____

I wasn't at school. There were two _____

starfish. There wasn't a shark. _____

6 Gadgets

 $200

 $22

1 Look and complete the words.

g a m e
c o n s o l e

e_ _ _ _ _ r_ _
f_ _ _

 $25

 $12

 $90

w_ _ _ _ _ e –
_ _ _ _ _ e

e_ _ _ _ _ _ _ _
t_ _ t_ _ _ _ _ _

t_ _ _ e_ _

 $8

 $345

$325

_ l_ _ _ _ l_ _ _ _ t

c_ _ l
p_ _ _ _ _

_ _ p_ _ p

e_ _ _ _ _ t_ _

2 Look at Activity 1. Read and write the prices.

1 **A:** Hello, can I help you?
   B: Yes, I'd like a laptop, please.
   A: That's $ __325__.

2 **A:** Hello, can I help you?
   B: Yes, I'd like a game console, please.
   A: That's $_____.

3 **A:** Hello, can I help you?
   B: Yes, I'd like a flashlight and an electric toothbrush, please.
   A: That's $_____.

4 **A:** Hello, can I help you?
   B: Yes, I'd like a tablet and a walkie-talkie, please.
   A: That's $_____.

3 Write a dialogue. Use items and prices from Activity 1.

A: Hello, can I help you?

B: Yes, I'd like _____.

A: That's $_____.

1 **Read and write the names of the items.**

1 _____   2 _____   3 _____   4 _____

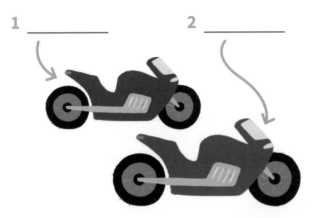 

The MX8 is bigger than the MX7.   The RS 5 is more expensive than the XT 10.

2 **Look and write the words.**

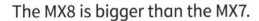

cheaper   expensive   ~~smaller~~   bigger

1 The Delta is __smaller__ than the Omega.

2 The Omega is _____ than the Delta.

3 The Omega is _____ than the Delta.

4 The Delta is more _____ than the Omega.

3 **Look and write about the dogs.**

__Mister is bigger than Lucky.__ _____

_____

_____

_____

1 **Remember the song. Correct the sentences.**

1 My gadget is smaller than yours.   My gadget is bigger than yours.

2 My gadget is uglier than yours.   _____

3 My gadget is older than yours.   _____

4 My gadget is cheaper than yours.   _____

2 **Look at the gadget. Write what happens when you press each button.**

flashlight
comes on

_____
comes on

_____
comes on

_____
comes on

3 **Complete the dialogues about the gadget from Activity 2.**

1 **A:** What happens when you press the **red**_____ button?

B: The **flashlight**_____ comes on. I use it to _____.

2 **A:** What happens when you press the _____ button?

B: The _____ comes on. I use it to _____.

3 **A:** What happens when you press the _____ button?

B: The _____ comes on. I use it to _____.

4 **A:** What happens when you press the _____ button?

B: The _____ comes on. I use it to _____.

1 Look, read, and write *t* (true) or *f* (false).

		price	weight	size
	Turbo 10	$14	200g	15cm
	Turbo 15	$22	225g	18cm
	Turbo 18	$30	175g	12cm

1 The Turbo 10 is the most expensive. [f]

2 The Turbo 15 is more expensive than the Turbo 18. [ ]

3 The Turbo 18 is the cheapest. [ ]

4 The Turbo 18 is smaller than the Turbo 15. [ ]

5 The Turbo 15 is the biggest. [ ]

6 The Turbo 10 is the heaviest. [ ]

2 Look at Activity 1. Write sentences.

1 cheap   The Turbo 10 is the cheapest.

2 big _____

3 small _____

4 heavy _____

5 expensive _____

3 Use the internet and write names or places.

the world's oldest woman …   🔍

1 the world's oldest woman _____

2 the world's most expensive car _____

3 the world's biggest swimming pool _____

4 the world's smallest house _____

5 the world's heaviest bird _____

1 🛡 **Read the story _The Cave_ again. Check ☑ the best answer.**

1 In picture 1, what does Ben mean when he says, "Somewhere down there …"?

A ☐ A place below a tree.

B ☐ A place under a stone.

C ☑ A place in the caves.

2 In picture 3, why does Ben say, "The flashlight was a good idea."?

A ☐ Because he's scared of the dark.

B ☐ Because it's dark in the cave.

C ☐ Because a flashlight is his favorite gadget.

3 In picture 6, how does Lucy know Horax and Zelda are in the caves?

A ☐ Buster sees them.

B ☐ She sees them.

C ☐ Ben tells her.

4 Who makes the noise in the cave?

A ☐ Horax and Zelda.

B ☐ Buster.

C ☐ Ben.

2 🖐 🛡 **Read the story below. What can we learn from it? Check ☑ or X ☒.**

☐ Always ask your parents for help with ideas.

☐ Use your imagination.

☐ Giving is better than taking.

Jake: Oh, no. There isn't any paper for me.

Nicole: Don't worry. I have an idea.

Jake: Thanks, Nicole. It looks great.

Dad: Where's the front page of my paper?

1 🎧 024 **Listen and write the missing words. Then say with a friend.**

Burglar 1: I'm going in.

Burglar 2: Hurry up. Don't be too long.

Burglar 1: I won't. _____ _____ _____ _____.

Burglar 2: OK. Don't worry.

Police officer: Hello, gentlemen. Can I help you?

Explorer 1: Oh, no! We have a problem.

Explorer 2: Don't worry. _____ _____ _____ _____.

Explorer 1: What is it?

Explorer 2: Run!

2 **Write the words in the table.**

phone   use   ~~Irene~~   game   nine   cheese   computer   code   rain   light   coat   time   play   really   music

say	see	five	go	you
	Irene			

3 🎧 025 **Listen, say, and check your answers.**

1 🎧 **026** **Listen and write the names under the pictures. There are three extra pictures.**

Jenny~~ Tim   Olivia

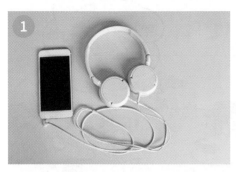

_____

Jenny

_____

2 **Read the text. Choose the right words and write them on the lines.**

GAME CONSOLES

There are many game consoles that we __can__ play with. The **(1)** _____ game console is more than 40 years old! It's bigger **(2)** _____ the ones we have today. It is slower, too. Modern consoles are smaller and faster. You can play games on these consoles and **(3)** _____ DVDs, too. Some game consoles also connect to the internet. Game consoles are not very cheap. Today, the **(4)** _____ expensive game consoles cost around $600, and the cheapest ones cost about $50. Many people like game consoles because the games **(5)** _____ fun and many people can play together with one console.

Example	can	do	let's
1	old	young	oldest
2	more	than	the
3	watch	have	open
4	more	most	than
5	are	is	do

1 **Look, read, and write.**

Examples

The biggest boy is talking on his __cell phone__ .

What does the boy in the blue T-shirt have? __a flashlight__

Complete the sentences.

1 There are _____ balls in the yard.

2 The boy in the red T-shirt is bigger than the boy in the blue _____ .

Answer the questions.

3 Where is the bicycle? _____ .

4 What do the boys in the gray T-shirts have? _____
_____ .

Now write two sentences about the picture.

5 _____ .

6 _____ .

CAVE PAINTINGS

1 **Look and write the words. Then complete the sentences.**

rock powder   lamp   cave ceiling   twig   ~~charcoal~~

charcoal _____ _____ _____ _____

1 Artists still use __charcoal__ to draw pictures.

2 I drew a picture with a _____ from a tree in our art class today.

3 Cave artists used _____ to make colored paint.

4 We saw some bats sleeping on the _____.

5 Dad had an old oil _____ so we could see in the dark.

2 **Look at these cave paintings. Then read and match.**

1 This painting is in the Sahara Desert. It shows a man with a tall giraffe. It tells us that giraffes are thousands of years old and live in the desert.

2 This painting tells us how people traveled. Some people are on camels, and some are walking. This picture is from a cave in Algeria.

3 In this picture, we can see people hunting. Some people are talking, too. You can see this picture in a cave in Thailand.

3 Look at these pictures. Write the things the artists used to make them.

brushes ~~pencils~~ rock powder charcoal fingers and hands leaves

1

2

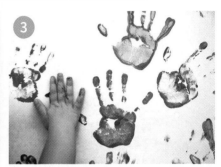
3

pencils
_____
_____

4

5

6

_____
_____
_____

4 Imagine you are an artist. Draw a picture. Write a paragraph about your picture.

I draw my pictures on _____

I use _____

In this picture you can see _____

_____
_____
_____
_____
_____
_____
_____
_____
_____
_____

1 🎧 **027** **Put the dialogue in order. Then listen and check.**

☐ **B:** Yes. Do you have any flashlights?

[1] **A:** Good morning. Can I help you?

☐ **A:** It's 14 dollars. The blue one is cheaper. It's only eight dollars.

☐ **B:** How much is the green one?

☐ **A:** Yes, we do. We have this blue flashlight and this green one.

☐ **B:** That's great. Can I buy the blue one, please?

☐ **A:** Of course!

☐ **B:** Thank you.

2 **Look and write a dialogue. Use language from Activity 1.**

Salesclerk: <u>Good morning. Can I help you?</u>

Girl: _____

_____

_____

_____

_____

What do I know?

1 Color the bricks to make sentences. Write in the missing words.

1	I'm	tallest	than the watch.
2	The flashlight	older than	faster _____ mine.
3	Mike's	beautiful dog	_____ in our class.
4	Jack is the	bike is	in the world.
5	It's the _____	is _____ expensive	my brother.

2 Read and think. Then write two more.

BIG QUESTION How are gadgets useful?

Gadgets can help us listen to music, play games,

_____, and _____.

About me!

3 Read. Then write about you and draw.

A gadget I use a lot is my tablet.   _____

It plays music when I press a button.   _____

It's faster than my old phone.   _____

1 Find eight words and write. Look ➡ and ⬇.

s	t	o	m	a	c	h	a	c	h	e
x	o	o	a	p	p	e	r	s	e	a
r	o	l	s	d	s	a	i	k	a	r
t	t	b	c	o	l	d	e	r	r	a
p	h	t	o	c	w	a	s	a	c	c
n	a	u	e	t	f	c	o	u	g	h
a	c	l	e	o	r	h	l	o	y	e
m	h	n	u	r	s	e	e	d	m	i
h	e	a	y	t	o	a	l	b	a	k

stomachache _____

_____ _____ _____

2 Remember the story. Match the sentences.

1 Ben gets a message.

2 He is in the hospital.

3 The children go to the hospital.

4 Ben and Lucy take the elevator.

a A nurse says he is in room 209, upstairs.

b A doctor shows them the room.

c It says his grandpa is sick.

d Ben wants to visit him.

3 Complete the dialogue.

What's the _____?

I have _____.

1 Write the words.

1 play   _played_

2 jump   _____

3 look at   _____

4 smile   _____

5 land   _____

6 shout   _____

7 learn   _____

8 listen to   _____

9 visit   _____

10 phone   _____

11 watch   _____

12 be   _____

2 Read and write the words. Change the words to talk about yesterday.

shout   ~~be~~   visit   be   listen   look   smile

Yesterday, my friend and I (1) __were__ in the park. Suddenly, there was this big, black dog.

Jonathan (2) _____ at its eyes.

"Go away!" he (3) _____.

On Sunday, Sue (4) _____ her grandma. Grandma (5) _____ very happy with the flowers and the cake. She (6) _____ a lot. Sue and her grandma (7) _____ to a piano concert together.

3 Look and write the story. Change the words to talk about Sunday.

~~watch~~   shout   jump   be

On Sunday I watched a soccer game

_____

_____

_____

_____

_____

_____

1 **Remember the song. Write the words.**

swallowed   walked   got   landed   looked up   ~~was~~   was   was

The girl **(1)** __was__ in the kitchen. There
(2) _____ a big apple cake in the kitchen,
too. She **(3)** _____ the big cake and then
(4) _____ a stomachache. She **(5)** _____
at a farm and **(6)** _____ at a snake. Then she
(7) _____ into a tree. At the market, a box of
apples **(8)** _____ on her knee. It was a bad day.

2 **Imagine you had a bad day. Write where you were and what happened.**

I was at the _____ .

_____ .

_____ .

3 **Complete this song. Use your ideas from Activity 2. Then draw.**

I was at the _____ .
I looked – there were _____ .
I _____ .
And now it really aches.

1 **Look at the letters. Write the words.**

			Simple Past	
1	kwae pu	wake up	woke up	
2	eelf			
3	asy			
4	og			
5	veig			
6	vhae			

2 **Complete the story. Use words from Activity 1.**

Last Saturday, Joe Freeze, the small ice-cream monster,

(1) <u>woke up at half past eight</u> . (2) _____ a

terrible headache. (3) _____ into his father's bedroom.

His father (4) _____ some medicine. Then Joe said,

"(5) _____?" "Of course," (6) _____.

Joe had some ice cream, and he (7) _____ better.

3 **Write three sentences about you. Use the words from Activity 1.**

1 <u>Last Sunday, I _____</u>.

2 <u>I _____</u>.

3 <u>I _____</u>.

1 **Read the story *At the Hospital* again. Write sentences.**

1 Lucy and Ben / go / hospital

   Lucy and Ben went to the hospital.

2 They / go / room 209

   _____

3 They / find / Horax, not / Ben / grandfather

   _____

4 It / be / trick

   _____

5 Horax / want / book and letters

   _____

6 At that moment / doctor / arrive

   _____

7 Ben / Lucy / say goodbye / and / go / out / room

   _____

2 **Write *t* (true) or *f* (false).**

1 The doctor takes Ben and Lucy to room 209. | t |

2 Ben's grandfather plays a trick on the children. | |

3 Horax wants the book from the children. | |

4 Lucy gives Horax the book. | |

5 The doctor thinks Horax is Ben's grandfather. | |

3 **How is Ben feeling? Look and number the pictures.**

1 He's scared.   2 He's happy.   3 He's surprised.

1 🎧 028 **Listen and write the missing words. Then say with a friend.**

Man: Oh, no! What happened to you?

Tom: I fell off my bike.

Man: _____ _____ _____?

Tom: I'm fine, but my bike isn't!

Fred: I want to play.

Katie: I'm busy. Can't you see?

Fred: But I'm bored. Please play with me.

Katie: _____ _____ _____!

2 🎧 029 **Listen and write the words in the table.**

~~liked~~   played   jumped   landed   shouted   smiled   wanted   listened   looked

walked /t/	phoned /d/	hated /id/
liked		

3 🎧 030 **Listen, say, and check your answers.**

1 🎧 **031** **Listen to Emma's story again. Check ✓ the correct sentences.**

1 Emma felt sick because she had a headache. ✓

2 She had an operation right away. ☐

3 Emma never walked again without crutches. ☐

4 The Helper Dog Project had dogs in wheelchairs. ☐

5 Jasper helped Emma walk again. ☐

6 Jasper got an important prize. ☐

2 🛡 **Complete the summary. Use the words from the box in the correct tense.**

feel   help   learn   ~~like~~   visit   remember   say

Emma **(1)** _liked_ swimming and riding her bike. Emma's headache got worse and worse, and she **(2)** _____ very sick. The doctor **(3)** _____ Emma needed an operation. After the operation, Emma couldn't remember how to do anything. She had to use a wheelchair or crutches. Emma didn't try to walk because she was very tired. One day, Emma and her parents **(4)** _____ the Helper Dog Project. One of the big dogs came to Emma and put his paw on Emma's leg. His name was Jasper. He and Emma became best friends. Jasper **(5)** _____ Emma, and she slowly **(6)** _____ to walk again with no crutches. Last week, a magazine gave Jasper a big prize: The Best Animal of the Year! Emma said to Jasper, "You are now the most famous dog in the world!" Jasper put his paw on Emma's leg. She **(7)** _____ the first time she saw Jasper and smiled.

3 🤲 🛡 **Read the story again and think. Color the circles green for *yes* or red for *no*.**

◯ You should stop trying.   ◯ Never give up.

1 Read and check ☑ the best answer. Emma is talking to the doctor.

1 Doctor: Hello, Emma. How are you?

   Emma: A ☑ I don't feel well this morning.

        B ☐ I'm watching a movie.

        C ☐ I'm Claire's sister.

2 Doctor: What's the matter? Do you have a stomachache?

   Emma: A ☐ No, thank you. I don't want one.

        B ☐ No, I have a headache.

        C ☐ Yes, thank you.

3 Doctor: Would you like some water?

   Emma: A ☐ Yes, I had some water this morning.

        B ☐ No, thanks. I'd like some orange juice.

        C ☐ Well, I like hamburgers a lot.

4 Doctor: Do you want a comic book?

   Emma: A ☐ Yes, please.

        B ☐ OK, it is.

        C ☐ Yes, I had.

5 Doctor: Can I give you some medicine?

   Emma: A ☐ He can give me one.

        B ☐ I can give you one.

        C ☐ Yes, I'd like that. Thanks.

KEEPING HEALTHY

1 **Look and match. Then complete the sentence.**

1 exercise   4 sleep

2 healthy food   5 rest

3 unhealthy food   6 fresh air

Healthy __food____, rest, getting _____, and getting _____ help us stay _____.

2 **Read and write the words. Use words from Activity 1.**

Hi Denise!

Last week, I decided to do more to stay (1) __healthy__. First, I changed what I eat. At lunch, I have a sandwich and an apple. For dinner, I have lots of fresh vegetables. I have some cake or chocolate, but not every day! So now I don't eat (2) _____ food. I also walk to school every day, and I joined a volleyball team last week. So, I (3) _____ more now. I also take the dog for a walk and ride my bike in the park. This way, I get lots of (4) _____.

In the evening, I watch TV or read a comic book. I also go to bed early during the week, so I'm not tired in the morning. It's important to get (5) _____ too.

Do you want to go swimming with me on Saturday?

Bye,

Dora

3 **Write the words from the box.**

~~get tired eyes~~   have a healthy diet   get fresh air
be tired in the morning   get good exercise

ACTIVITY		RESULT
1 playing computer games	→	get tired eyes
2 going to bed late	→	_____
3 walking to school	→	_____
4 swimming	→	_____
5 eating fruit and vegetables	→	_____

4 **Read and check ☑ the two that are healthy.**

1

I eat a lot of pizza and cake.
I love chips and bread.
Sometimes I have fruit.

☐

2

I go to bed early and exercise
every day. I sometimes watch
TV and rest.

☐

3

I sometimes eat chocolate,
but I always have fruit and
vegetables. I always exercise.

☐

5 **Write what you do to keep healthy.**

To keep healthy I _____

_____

_____

_____

1 Read and write *d* (doctor) or *p* (patient).

1 What's the matter? <u>d</u>

2 Do you have a headache? ___

3 When can I go to school again? ___

4 Do you have any other aches? ___

5 I'm so hot. Can I drink some cold orange juice? ___

6 What do I have? ___

2 Read the answers and write *d* (doctor) or *p* (patient). Then match them with the questions from Activity 1.

a ☐ Yes, but it's not bad. <u>P</u>

b ☐ I'm not sure. Maybe in a week. ___

c ☐ 1 I have a stomachache. ___

d ☐ Don't worry. It's nothing serious. But you have to rest. ___

e ☐ No, just the stomachache. ___

f ☐ You have to drink a lot, but you can't drink anything cold. ___

3 Look and write a dialogue. Use language from Activities 1 and 2.

Doctor: What's the matter?

Patient: _____

_____

_____

_____

_____

1 Look and draw lines to make sentences.

1 I

plays	soccer	at school	with my sister.
played	tennis	in the park	with my brother.
playing	volleyball	on the beach	with my dad.

2 She

waked up	at	three o'clock	this morning.
woke up	on	five o'clock	this night.
wake up	in	six o'clock	this evening.

3 She

feeling sick,	she so	go to	the doctor's.
felt sick,	so she	goes to	bed.
feel sick,	because she	went to	school.

2 Read and think. Then write two more sentences.

BIG QUESTION What keeps us healthy?

Getting fresh air keeps us healthy.

_____

_____

3 Read. Then write about you and draw.

Last week I went to the doctor's. I had a headache and a toothache. I felt bad.

_____

_____

_____

8 Around the World

1 Match the letters and write the countries. Then match the countries with the flags.

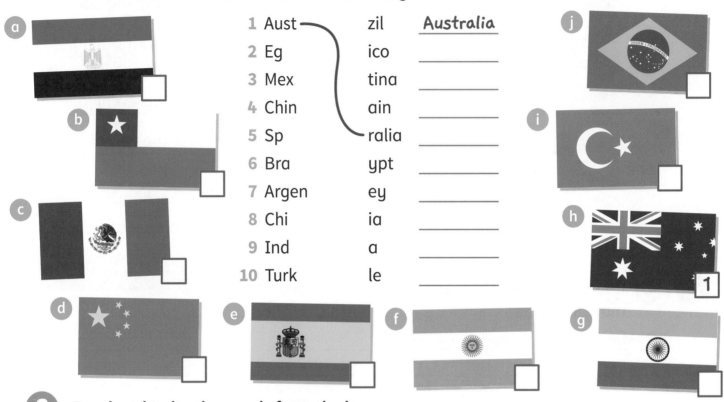

1	Aust	zil	_Australia_
2	Eg	ico	_____
3	Mex	tina	_____
4	Chin	ain	_____
5	Sp	ralia	_____
6	Bra	ypt	_____
7	Argen	ey	_____
8	Chi	ia	_____
9	Ind	a	_____
10	Turk	le	_____

a b c d e f g h i j

1

2 Read and write the words from the box.

> enjoy   visit   country   change   choose   ~~tickets~~   are

Ben: Two (1) _tickets_ for the park, please.

Assistant: That's $4.

Lucy: Here you (2) _____. $5.

Assistant: Thank you. Your tickets and your (3) _____. (4) _____ the model town.

Ben: Thanks.

Lucy: Come on, Ben. Which (5) _____ do you want to (6) _____ first?

Ben: I don't know. It's so difficult to (7) _____.

3 Complete the sentence. Then draw and color.

My country is _____. This is my flag.

1 Match and color.

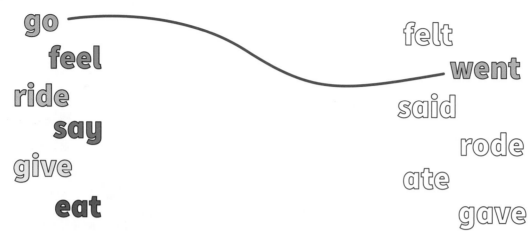

go
feel
ride
say
give
eat

felt
went
said
rode
ate
gave

2 Circle the correct words.

1 We went to the beach, but we **not** / (**didn't**) go swimming.

2 We rode an elephant in the zoo, but we **didn't** / **don't** ride a horse.

3 I saw Bill at the birthday party, but I **doesn't** / **didn't** see Harry.

4 They gave the horse an apple, but they **not gave** / **didn't give** him any candy.

5 She said a lot, but she **didn't** / **isn't** say her name.

6 He ate all the chocolate, but he **didn't eat** / **not ate** the ice cream.

3 Complete the sentences.

Jack   Ruby   Charlie

Ella   Lucas   Grace

1 Jack watched TV, but _he didn't feel scared_ .

2 Ruby saw lots of elephants, but _____ .

3 Charlie played soccer in the park, but _____ .

4 Ella ate lots of oranges, but _____ .

5 Lucas went to the swimming pool, but _____ .

6 Grace went to Spain, but _____ .

1 🛡 **Remember the song. Circle the correct words.**

1 I went to (China) / **India**, but I didn't see the wall.

2 In India, I didn't see the **sun** / **Taj Mahal**.

3 I went to Egypt, but I didn't see the **lynx** / **Sphinx**.

4 I went to **Australia** / **Brazil**, but I didn't see the sun.

5 In Brazil, I didn't see the **wall** / **Amazon**.

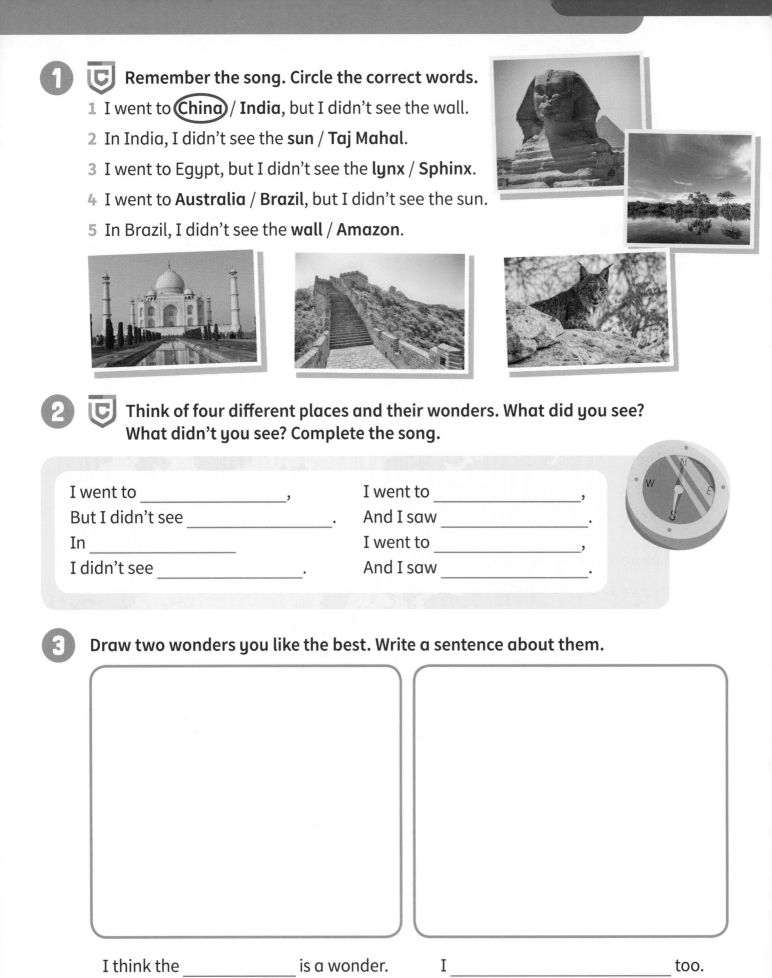

2 🛡 **Think of four different places and their wonders. What did you see? What didn't you see? Complete the song.**

I went to _____ ,   I went to _____ ,

But I didn't see _____ .   And I saw _____ .

In _____   I went to _____ ,

I didn't see _____ .   And I saw _____ .

3 **Draw two wonders you like the best. Write a sentence about them.**

I think the _____ is a wonder.   I _____ too.

1 Put the words in order.

1 did / on / vacation / where / go / you / ?

<u>Where did you go on vacation?</u>

2 you / fun / have / there / did / ?

_____

3 Mexico / long / did / stay / how / you / in / ?

_____

4 where / stay / did / you / ?

_____

5 go / did / museum / you / a / there / to / ?

_____

6 buy / me / a / you / did / present / ?

_____

2 Look and write answers. 😊 = yes ☹ = no

1 Did you do a lot of shopping in London? 😊

<u>Yes, I did.</u>

2 Did he see the Pyramids? ☹

_____

3 Did she buy lots of postcards? ☹

_____

4 Did they have a good time? 😊

_____

5 Did you go to the zoo? ☹

_____

6 Did they eat lots of pizza? 😊

_____

1 Read the story *The Final Letters* again. Put the lines in order.

☐ Then they look at the Great Wall of China, but they can't see the missing letters.

☐ After that, they look at the Sydney Opera House.

☐ They want to look for their book.

☑ 1 First, Lucy and Ben look at a soccer stadium in Brazil.

☐ They see that they don't have the book.

☐ Finally, Lucy finds the missing letters.

☐ Then they see Mr. Williams, the librarian.

☐ Ben says that he is hungry.

2 🖐 🛡 Read the story below. What can we learn from it? Draw 😃 or 🙁.

◯ It's interesting to try food from another culture.

◯ Eat only what you really know.

In a restaurant ...

Mom: Let's try some food from Turkey.
         Would you like some spinach and potatoes?

Oliver: No, Mom.

Mom: What about some rice with peas or beans?

Oliver: I'm not sure. Can I have a hamburger?

The next day after school ...

Oliver: Adil, I'm hungry. Let's get a hamburger.

Adil: Oliver, I don't like hamburgers. Come to my house, we can have dinner there.

Oliver: OK, but I have to call my mom from your house.

At Adil's house ...

Adil: Yummy! Rice with peas, beans, potatoes, and spinach. I hope you like it, Oliver.

Oliver: Mmm. It's very good, Mrs. Demir.

Adil's mom: Thank you, Oliver.

Two days later ...

Oliver: Mom, I'm hungry. Can I have some spinach with potatoes, please?

1 🎧 032 **Listen and write the missing words. Then say with a friend.**

Jenny: Be careful. That's Mom's favorite vase.

Ben: I know. I am being careful.

Jenny: OK, but _____ _____ _____.

Ben: OK. Now can you just get out of my ...

Jenny: Oh, no!

Connor: What are you looking for, Izzie?

Izzie: My pen. I had it a minute ago. Now it's gone.

Connor: That's strange.

Izzie: I know. _____ _____ _____ _____?

Connor: Why don't you look behind your ear, Izzie?

2 **Look and write the words.**

dry   Turkey   ~~pyramid~~   yuck   happy   buy   Egypt   young

it	very	five	yellow
pyramid			

3 🎧 033 **Listen, say, and check your answers.**

1 Look and read. Write 1, 2, or 3 words to complete the sentences about the story.

Last month, Max and his parents went on vacation to Chile. They went by plane to Easter Island. Then they went by car and visited some big rocks. The rocks looked like people. Max and Dad took some photos. In the afternoon Max was very hot. "Can we go swimming, Mom?" "I'm not sure. What does the sign say?"

Max opened the car door and ran to the beach. He didn't read the sign. His mom ran to the beach, too. She read the sign and saw some trash. "Max! Please come out! You can't swim in this water!" Max came out of the water. Max dried himself. Then they went back to the car and drove on.

After an hour, they came to a town. They had dinner there, but Max didn't eat anything. He felt sick. He had a stomachache.
The next day Max was very sick. They went to the doctor's, and the doctor gave Max some pills. Poor Max felt sick for three days. Max said to his parents, "I swam in the ocean. I didn't read the sign. I wasn't very smart."

1 The family __went__ on vacation to Chile.

2 They _____ big rocks that looked like people.

3 Max wanted to go swimming because it _____ very hot.

4 Max ran to the beach, but he _____ read the sign.

5 There was some trash on the _____.

6 Max _____ anything to eat at the restaurant.

7 Max was _____ for three days.

8 Max said not reading the sign wasn't _____.

1 🎧 034 **Listen and write. There is one example.**

The Time Machine

Lily went to: South _Africa_

1 She showed the people she was: _____

2 Food she ate: _____

3 The beach was very: _____

4 She stayed for one or two: _____

2 **Look and write about David's trip in the time machine.**

David visited Greenland in the
time machine.
_____
_____
_____
_____
_____
_____
_____

Wonders of the World

1 Read about the wonders of the world again. Check ☑ the correct sentences.

1 There are pink snakes in the Grand Canyon. ☑

2 The beaches next to the Harbor of Rio de Janeiro are small. ☐

3 The Northern Lights can be more than one color. ☐

4 Mount Everest isn't very old. ☐

5 Many fish live in the Great Barrier Reef. ☐

6 The Zambezi River forms a big waterfall. ☐

2 Match the natural wonders with the texts.

> Harbor of Rio de Janeiro   Victoria Falls   ~~Great Barrier Reef~~

1 Great Barrier Reef

Apart from different species of fish, you can also see whales and dolphins here. There are also 900 different islands around it and more than 2,500 reefs. It is in danger because of ocean pollution and climate change.

2 _____

It is named after a famous English queen. The area has a dry season and a rainy season. When it rains, more than 300,000 gallons of water fall there every second. When it doesn't rain, you can walk across the top. You can swim there, too.

3 _____

There are more than 100 islands here with 15 different cities. There are 30 different beaches here, too, and in summer, a million people can be on the beaches at the same time.

3 Write about one more natural wonder.

_____
_____
_____
_____

4 **What do you know about these man-made wonders? Do the quiz. Circle the answers.**

KNOW YOUR WONDERS

1 The Great Pyramid is in …
a Cairo   b Giza   c Khufu

2 The Pyramid was the tallest building until …
After that, Lincoln Cathedral in England was the tallest in 1311.
a 1310   b 1312   c 755

3 The longest wall in the world is called the …
a Grand Canyon   b Great Wall   c Grand Wall

4 The wall has more than … stones.
a 2.3 billion   b 2,300   c 2.3 million

5 The Taj Mahal was built to remember …
a a wife   b a daughter   c Shah Jahan

6 The palace is in …
a Australia   b Argentina   c India

5 🛡 **Imagine you are going to make a wonder for this world. Write about it. Then draw.**

- what it is
- where it is
- why you are making it
- what it looks like

_____

_____

_____

_____

_____

_____

1 Match the questions with the answers.

1 Lucas, where did you go in your time machine?
2 What did you see?
3 Did you have fun?
4 Was it hot?
5 How long did you stay there?
6 Did you buy anything?

a Yes, it was. But I was OK. I had a big hat.
b I went to ancient Egypt.
c No, I didn't, but I took some photos.
d I saw the pyramids. There were thousands of people working there.
e Yes, I did. It was great.
f About five hours.

2 Read about Lucas. Read and underline the mistakes. Then write the correct sentences.

Lucas went to ancient Egypt in his time machine. He saw the pyramids, but <u>he only saw three or four people</u>. He didn't have fun in Egypt. He had a big hat with him. He stayed in Egypt for about 15 hours. He bought some food and took some photos.

He saw thousands of people.

_____

_____

_____

3 Write about your travels in your time machine.

The time machine stopped. I was somewhere new.
But where was I? I opened the door of
my time machine, and I saw ...

1 Color the bricks to make sentences. Write in the missing words.

1	Did you	did you _____	vacation last year?
2	Where did	go_____ to London	your plane leave?
3	How long	_____ did	on the safari?
4	What	you go _____	in the hotel?
5	_____ you see	a lion	last week?

2 Read and think.
Then write two more.

BIG QUESTION What wonders of the world are there?

The Northern Lights, Mount Everest, Paricutin Volcano,

_____, _____.

 3 Read. Then write about you and draw.

Last year I went on vacation
to Spain. I stayed in a hotel.
I saw a beautiful beach.

_____

_____

_____

9 Vacation Plans

1 Read the clues and do the crossword puzzle. Find the secret word.

1 When there's lots of rain and lightning. You can hear big "bangs."

2 You use this in the rain.

3 A good day to fly your kite.

4 A flash from the sky.

5 When you can't see the sun.

6 When you can't see where you are going.

7 You can get very wet in weather like this.

8 You put these on your feet when it's raining.

Crossword grid (Down answer): ¹t h u n d e r s t o r m

2 Read and write words from the crossword puzzle in Activity 1.

The weather was terrible yesterday. It was cold and (1) _foggy_ in the morning. Then there was no sun because it was (2) _____. At lunchtime, it was very (3) _____, so all my things got wet. And then at about 5 o'clock, the (4) _____ started. There was lots of (5) _____ in the sky. I was scared because I was in a tent, camping! And I didn't have an (6) _____ or a (7) _____ to wear. And I didn't have any (8) _____ for my feet. It was awful!

3 Write about the weather last week.

On Monday, it was _____ in the morning. On Wednesday, it was _____.

On Friday, it was _____

On _____

_____

_____

1 Look, read, and check ☑ or correct the sentences.

Monday	Tuesday	Wednesday	Thursday	Friday	Saturday

1 On Monday, it's going to be sunny.   cloudy

2 On Tuesday, it isn't going to be rainy. _____

3 On Wednesday, it's going to be sunny. _____

4 On Thursday, it's going to be foggy.   _____

5 On Friday, it's going to be cloudy.   _____

6 On Saturday, it's going to be rainy.   _____

2 Match to make a diary. Then write sentences.

Monday   [e]

Tuesday   [ ]

Wednesday [ ]

Thursday [ ]

Friday   [ ]

Saturday [ ]

a   b   c

d   e   f

1 On Monday, I'm going to watch TV _____.

2 On Tuesday, _____.

3 On Wednesday, _____.

4 On Thursday, _____.

5 On Friday, _____.

6 On Saturday, _____.

3 Write about your week.
Use *I'm going to* and *I'm not going to*.

On Monday, I'm going to ...

_____

1 Read the song again and correct the sentences.

1 I'm going to get up early.

I'm going to <u>stay in bed</u>_____.

2 I'm going to read my science book.

I'm going to _____.

3 I'm not going to travel far away.

I'm going to _____.

4 I'm going to walk in the rain.

I'm going to _____.

5 We aren't going to go back to school.

We're going to _____.

6 We're going to see our friends before our vacation.

We're going to _____.

2 Think about your vacation. Write and draw three things you're going to do.

I'm going to _____.

_____
_____
_____
_____
_____
_____
_____
_____

3 Write a verse for the song about you. Use your ideas from Activity 2.

I'm going to _____

And _____.

Then I'm going to _____.

I'm going to have lots of fun.

1 Put the words in order. Then look and answer.

1 you / are / to / France / going / visit / ... / ... ?

<u>Are you going to visit France?</u>   <u>No, I'm not.</u>

2 you / photos / take / going / are / to / ... / ... ?

_____   _____

3 you / go / snorkeling / are / going / to / ... / ... ?

_____   _____

4 going / are / to / music / listen / you / to / ... / ... ?

_____   _____

5 you / read / to / are / book / going / a / ... / ... ?

_____   _____

6 you / food / of / to / eat / are / going / lots / ... / ... ?

_____   _____

2 Answer the questions about you.

1 Are you going to do homework this evening? _____

2 Are you going to go swimming this weekend? _____

3 What are you going to do after school? _____

4 Are you going to visit your grandparents this weekend? _____

5 Are you going to go to bed early tonight? _____

6 What are you going to do this weekend? _____

1 🛡 Remember the story *The Treasure*. Write the words.

hear   treasure   friends   message   glasses   ~~castle~~   finders

Ben and Lucy go to the **(1)** _castle_ . They see Horax and Zelda near a door.
The door has a **(2)** _____ with a missing word above it. Horax and Zelda need
the letters. They **(3)** _____ Ben, and they get the children. Ben gives Zelda the
letters. Buster pulls off Horax's **(4)** _____ . Horax is Mr. Williams, the librarian!
Horax makes the word **(5)** "_____," and Zelda writes it above the door. Horax
and Zelda try to go in, but they can't. Ben and Lucy make the word **(6)** "_____."
They go in and find the **(7)** _____ .

2 Make words with the letters of *friendship*.

friends, finders, find ...
_____

3 Use the code to make words. Ask your friends to guess.

A	B	C	D	E	F	G	H	I	J	K	L	M	N	O	P	Q	R	S	T	U	V	W	X	Y	Z
☿	⚹	☉	ℂ	♊	♌	○	⚚	⊼	♀	◐	✳	◲	☽	♈	♉	♇	�})	≋	♌	♎	●	♃	∝	♂

_____ _____ _____ _____

4 🛡 Use the code to read more about the statue.

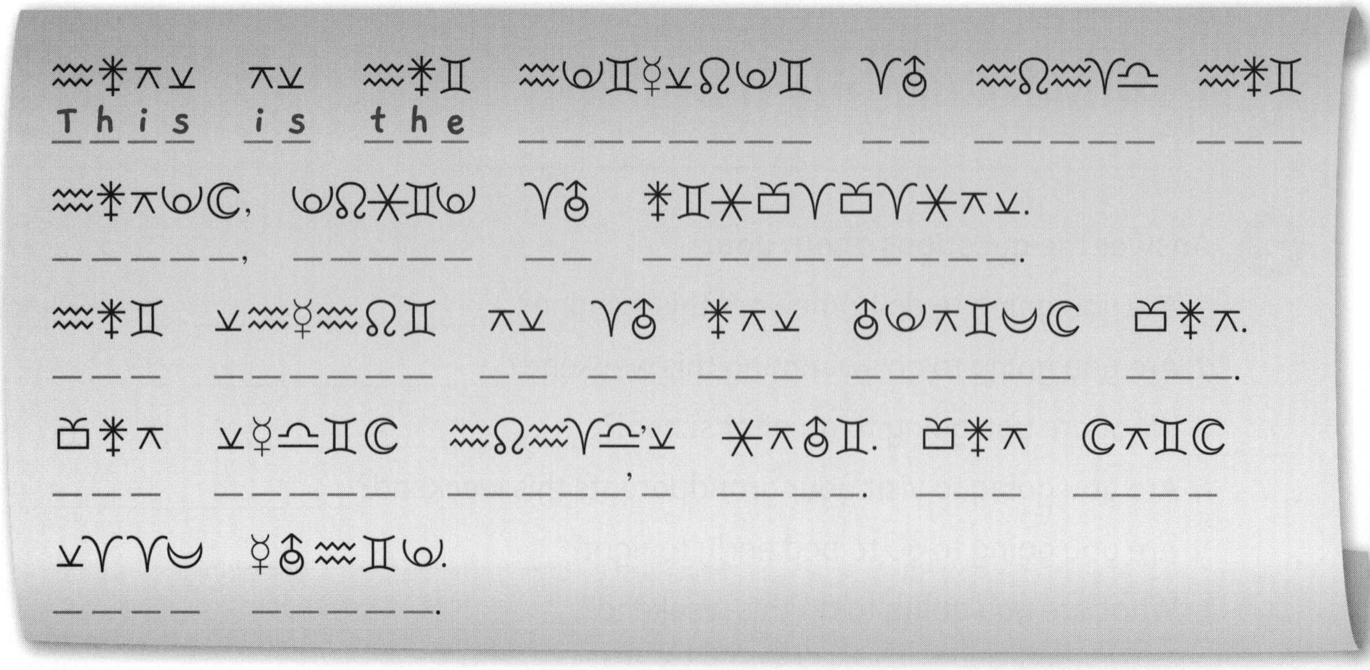

This is the _____ __ _____ ___

_____, _____ __ _____.

___ _____ __ __ ___ _____ ___.

___ _____ _____,_ _____. ___ ____

____ _____.

1 🎧 **035** **Listen and write the missing words. Then say with a friend.**

Ana: Are you sure you know what you're doing?

Jim: Of course I am. I do this all the time.

Ana: Look. _____ _____!

Jim: That's strange. Maybe the computer is broken.

Ana: It wasn't, but it is now!

Dad: Don't look at me like that …

It's my dinner. Now _____ _____!

Don't do that. I really don't like it when you do that.

… Oh, OK. You win. Here you go.

2 **Look and write *er, ar, ur,* or *ir*.**

1 th _i_ _r_ sty   **2** b __ __ thday   **3** n __ __ se   **4** Th __ __ sday

5 p __ __ fect   **6** g __ __ l   **7** t __ __ tle   **8** E __ __ th

3 🎧 **036** **Listen and say.**

1 Read Liam's story again.
Complete the summary.

| boring don't fantastic game |
| going rain thunderstorm ~~was~~ |

Liam was very excited because he

(1) _was_____ going to Florida

for two weeks. "It's going to be

(2) _____!" he said. "We can go for boat rides!" said Dad. "We can relax

and have a lot of fun!" said Mom. They arrived in Florida, and the hotel was beautiful.

"Tomorrow, I'm **(3)** _____ to swim in the ocean!" he said. But in the

middle of the night there was a lot of noise and Liam woke up. He looked outside

and saw a big **(4)** _____. Dad turned on the TV. "There's going to

be a lot of **(5)** _____ in Florida for the next fourteen days," said the

man on TV. "It's our vacation. We can't swim or see fish in the rain! It's going to be

(6) _____," Liam said. "We can have fun in our room. We can read, play

games, and listen to music," said Mom.

Two weeks later, their vacation was finished. "I **(7)** _____ want to go

home, Mom," Liam said. "It was a beautiful vacation!"

"Let's play another **(8)** _____," said Mom. Dad went to get their games

box. "Hooray!" shouted Liam.

2 Write *t* (true) or *f* (false).

1 The hotel was near the ocean. | t |

2 Liam wanted to swim in the rain. | ☐ |

3 It was going to be hot and sunny for fourteen days. | ☐ |

4 Liam thought the vacation was going to be boring in the rain. | ☐ |

5 Liam and his parents did many interesting things in their hotel room. | ☐ |

6 Liam didn't have fun on his vacation. | ☐ |

3 Read the story again and think. Color the circles green for *yes* or red
for *no*.

○ It's upsetting when plans change.

○ Try new things. You might really enjoy them.

1 Find differences. Circle them in picture 2.

2 Now write sentences about the differences.

In picture 1, the girl is holding an umbrella, but in picture 2 she's holding an ice cream cone.

VACATIONS IN THE PAST

1 Look and check ☑ what people had 100 years ago.

2 Complete the letter with the words from the box.

> swimming boots   picnic basket   puppet show
> donkey rides   crowded   ~~steam train~~   cart

June 2, 1922

Dear Elsa,

Thank you for your letter. You asked what I did on my vacation last week. Well, we went to Brighton beach.
The **(1)** **steam train** was comfortable but very noisy. It is better than traveling by horse though.
There were so many people at the beach – it was very **(2)** _____. I was upset because
I bought new **(3)** _____ but I couldn't wear them! We couldn't have a picnic there either,
so we went to Victoria Park. Mom brought a **(4)** _____ filled with sandwiches, lemonade,
and fruit. Then Uncle Joe bought us some ice cream from the **(5)** _____. It was delicious.

In the afternoon, we saw a **(6)** _____ with Punch and Judy, and I liked it. I didn't go on
the **(7)** _____ because I'm afraid of them.

We are going to take the train to Manchester to see Aunt Emma next week.
Are you going to be there?

Yours truly,

Sandra

3 **Look and read. Underline the things that are the same today.**

People started going on vacations after the 1850s. This is because the steam train made it easier to travel. The most popular place to go was the beach. There were donkey rides and <u>puppet shows</u>, but there were also theater shows, music halls, and even zoos.

Children made sandcastles on the beach and played different games. People sat on the beach and had picnics, too. They walked along the beach, but people didn't wear shorts and T-shirts. The beaches were very crowded.

People wore bathing suits that covered most of their bodies. Before going into the ocean, they got into a bathing carriage and changed from their ordinary clothes into their bathing suits. A horse pulled the carriage into the ocean, and then the swimmers dived into the water. Men and women didn't swim together.

4 **Imagine you are on vacation in the past. Write three things about it.**

- Where were you?
- How did you travel there?
- What did you do there?

_____

_____

_____

_____

_____

1 🎧 **037** **Put the dialogue in order. Then listen and check.**

[ ] **B:** I don't want to go to a city. There are too many people and cars.

[ ] **A:** I would like to go to the beach.

[1] **A:** Let's go on vacation.

[ ] **A:** No beach, no mountains, no cities. Let's just stay here!

[ ] **B:** Staying in the sun all day? No, that's boring.

[ ] **B:** Yes, that's a good idea. Where would you like to go?

[ ] **B:** Walking up and down all the time? No, thanks.

[ ] **A:** OK, so no mountains. We could go to a big city.

[ ] **A:** OK, no beach. What about the mountains?

2 🛡 **Look and write a dialogue. Use language from Activity 1.**

Boy: Where do you want to go on vacation?

Girl: _____

_____

_____

_____

_____

_____

What do I know?

1 Look and draw lines to make sentences.

1

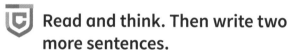

We

is going	to playing	tennis	tomorrow.
are going	play	soccer	yesterday.
am going	to play	computer games	last night.

2

I

is going	to call	to you	tonight
are going	calling	you	yesterday evening.
am going	to calling	your	last week.

3

Is

he	going	raining	tomorrow?
it	go to	rain	yesterday?
you	going to	rainy	last weekend?

2 Read and think. Then write two more sentences.

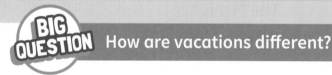

BIG QUESTION How are vacations different?

People traveled by steam train. They didn't wear sunglasses.

_____

_____

About me!

3 Read. Then write about you and draw.

On Saturday, I'm going to swim
in the ocean. I'm not going to sleep
all day.

_____

_____

_____

My Super Mind

1 Our School
Color your favorite activities.

- singing the song
- reading the Explorers story
- reading *Puzzles Are Great Fun*
- learning about geometric shapes
- finding out about our favorite subjects
- making my portfolio

Word Focus Write three new words.

_____ _____ _____

Language Focus Write two sentences about you.

_____

_____

Now tell a friend what you like and don't like in Unit 1.

---

2 The Picnic
Color your favorite activities.

- singing the song
- reading the Explorers story
- learning about edible plants
- acting out our sandwich store play
- drawing and writing about meals

Word Focus Write three new words.

_____ _____ _____

Language Focus Write two sentences about you.

_____

_____

Now tell a friend what you like and don't like in Unit 2.

---

3 Daily Tasks
Color your favorite activities.

- singing the song
- reading the Explorers story
- reading *The Shoemaker and the Elves*
- learning about jobs at night
- finding out about helping at home
- writing a poem

Word Focus Write three new words.

_____ _____ _____

Language Focus Write two sentences about you.

_____

_____

Now tell a friend what you like and don't like in Unit 3.

4 Around Town

Color your favorite activities.

- singing the song
- reading the Explorers story
- learning about tall buildings
- acting out our directions play
- writing and answering messages

Write three new words.

_____ _____ _____

Language Focus Write two sentences about you.

_____

_____

Now tell a friend what you like and don't like in Unit 4.

5 Under the Ocean

Color your favorite activities.

- singing the song
- reading the Explorers story
- reading *Saved by Dolphins*
- learning about climate change and pollution
- finding out about our Saturday afternoon
- writing about an ocean creature

Word Focus Write three new words.

_____ _____ _____

Language Focus Write two sentences about you.

_____

_____

Now tell a friend what you like and don't like in Unit 5.

6 Gadgets

Color your favorite activities.

- singing the song
- reading the Explorers story
- learning about cave paintings
- acting out our shopping play
- drawing and writing about my favorite gadget

Word Focus Write three new words.

_____ _____ _____

Language Focus Write two sentences about you.

_____

_____

Now tell a friend what you like and don't like in Unit 6.

7 In the Hospital

Color your favorite activities.

| singing the song |
| reading *A New Best Friend* |
| acting out our play at the doctor's |
| reading the Explorers story |
| learning about staying healthy |
| drawing and writing a story |

Write three new words.

_____ _____ _____

Language Focus Write two sentences about you.

_____

_____

Now tell a friend what you like and don't like in Unit 7.

---

8 Around the World

Color your favorite activities.

| singing the song |
| learning about wonders of the world |
| reading the Explorers story |
| finding out about our vacations |
| drawing and writing about a country |

Word Focus Write three new words.

_____ _____ _____

Language Focus Write two sentences about you.

_____

_____

Now tell a friend what you like and don't like in Unit 8.

---

9 Vacation Plans

Color your favorite activities.

| singing the song |
| reading *A Very Different Vacation* |
| acting out our vacation plans role play |
| reading the Explorers story |
| learning about vacation in the past |
| writing an email |

Word Focus Write three new words.

_____ _____ _____

Language Focus Write two sentences about you.

_____

_____

Now tell a friend what you like and don't like in Unit 9.